WILLIAM RUSCOE

A MANUAL FOR THE
POTTER

LONDON / Alec Tiranti / 1963

CONTENTS

1st edition 1948
2nd revised and enlarged edition 1959, 1963
PRINTED BY PORTLAND PRESS LTD.
BOUND BY C. & H. T. EVANS

© *Alec Tiranti Ltd., 72 Charlotte Street, London, W.1*

Made and printed in the United Kingdom

Preface

THIS book is written in the sincere hope that it may be of some use to the artist-potter student, and teacher of the craft. It may also be of interest to the industrial designer needing a background of processes and technique, to the layman seeking a more intimate knowledge of pottery making (for we are all users of pottery if not actual makers) and in the sphere of occupational therapy where its remedial value has proved of the greatest service.

The book is the result of some thirty-five years' experience, with first-hand knowledge of the various processes and methods used. The connection between the individual craftsman and the industrial worker has been stressed, for in pottery making each is a craftsman in his own particular right, and the machine tool has not entirely replaced the hand.

For artistic standards, I would refer the earnest student to the excellent examples in our museums. They are of every type and origin, a rich source of æsthetic values, and an inspiration to the potter.

Acknowledgements

Thanks are offered to Messers. William Boulton Ltd., Engineers, Burslem, for permission to make drawings of Figs. 13, 14, 15, 29, 35, 50, 51, 53, 56, 62 and 68. For permission to reproduce photographic plates Nos. XXXIII and XXXIV, Messrs. Crompton Parkinson Ltd., Astor House, Aldwych, London, W.C.2, taken respectively at Messrs. Thos. Lawrence (Longton) Ltd., Stoke-on-Trent, and at Messrs. Ford & Sons, Burslem, Stoke-on-Trent. For plates XXXVI, XXXVII and XXXVIII, Messrs. The Susie Cooper Pottery Ltd., Crown Works, Burslem ; plate XXXIX, A. E. Gray & Co. Ltd., Whieldon Road, Stoke-on-Trent. Plate XL, Messrs. Mr. R. G. Haggar, 'Ronson', Stone Road, Hanford, Stoke-on-Trent, and Messrs. Josiah Wedgwood & Sons Ltd., Barlaston, Staffordshire ; also for plate XLI to Mr. R. G. Haggar. The above photographs and plate XXXV were the work of Mr. Frank Nagington of Messrs. W. H. Nagington & Son Ltd., Hope Street, Hanley, Stoke-on-Trent. For permission to reproduce plate XLII, the Museum, Exeter. Plates XXV to XXIX and XXXI, XXXII were taken by kind permission of Mr. T. D. Murphy, Sandygate Pottery Ltd., Kingsteignton, Devon, and are the work of Mr. Max Peterkin of Exeter, as also are plates I to XXII and plate XXX. I am also indebted to Messrs. H. Howlett and Sons, Kiln Builders for assistance with the designs of the kilns and to Mr. Haggar for valuable suggestions and material in the text. Lastly to Mr. Alec Tiranti for his constructive help and assistance at all times.

Introduction

The art of the potter is one of the oldest of all the arts, for man has made vessels and small sculptures of baked clay since prehistoric times. The earliest pottery was simply dried in the sun, but the discovery that clay could be hardened by fire, and the later knowledge of glass rendering the porous pot impervious to moisture, gave man a fine imperishable material capable of strength, beauty and great artistic expression.

During the best periods of the past, pottery was made both by the individual craftsman or small group working collectively, as well as by the large team working under factory-like conditions. Greek and Chinese potters must have worked in both these manners.

The manner of making pottery has undergone little change, fundamentally, since the early times, except that in the case of factory-made wares, more mechanical means and reproductive methods are now employed, but the principles underlying these are the same. Clay still requires the intimate touch of the hand and expert skill at every stage. The most mechanical potter's wheel is still based on the primitive wheel of the peasant potter and modern kilns, though much larger and more efficient, are basically the same. Some of the world's most beautiful and exquisite pots must have been produced with rudimentary equipment, the disadvantage of which was offset by the loving care and great skill of the craftsman.

The twentieth century has brought its own particular problems and demands. These are partly met by specialist process workers and mass production methods; yet there is an increasing demand for the individual work of the artist and intimate expression of the craftsman. By the very nature of the craft, pottery lends itself more than any other manual art, to such demands.

It must be pointed out that some of the modern industrial methods have been adopted not because the processes offered artistic possibilities, but because they were capable of being exploited to imitate older processes at a much cheaper price. The artistic possibilities of the new processes were not always seen, but lately it has been realised that mass production methods are legitimate, provided that the method is not imitative but conforms to its own æsthetics. Too often, however, forms made by hand methods, were adapted to the machines instead of the peculiar limitations of the machine being recognised and specially designed for. This could only lead to gradual deterioration.

In the first place we had thrown forms, which were functional with truly wheel-made characteristics with good pulled handles and adequate spouts; later, moulded forms which were clean and precise but degenerated into softened and blurred forms. Lastly we have machine-made goods by completely automatic machinery. In the decorating process, painting was imitated by overglaze engraved transfers (filled in by hand)

and chromo-lithography in imitation of painting, with or without hand-touching, followed by photo-lithographic transfers. The washing-in of ground colours by brushwork was superseded by ground-laying only, to be followed by aerographed colour. Rubber stamping in gold eliminated the gilding by hand, and the shallow engraved plates economised in the quantity of gold used. Direct brushwork decoration led to *pounced* outlines brushed in, followed by the silk screen stencil.

All this had led to a gradual artistic and technical deterioration, but there is no reason why chromo-lithography or any of the other methods should not be used in an interesting manner. The process matters but little, it is the use to which it is put that is important if we are to achieve that standard of excellence to be seen in the best works of the past.

I. Nature of clays and bodies

The essential characteristic of clay is plasticity in the wet state, a quality which it loses temporarily on drying, and permanently when fired. Clays are decomposed rocks colloidal in nature which upon being burned return to something like their original rocky state. The term *clay* is used when natural clays are indicated, and *bodies* (or *paste*) when a composition of one or more natural clays is used together with crushed rocks and minerals. Natural clays are seldom used alone, as few are satisfactory in themselves, being either too plastic, or insufficiently plastic, and do not possess the three definite properties which successful pottery-making demands. The most important is, of course, plasticity, for without this the shapes could not be formed, whether by hand or mould. The second is porosity ; highly plastic clays can easily be shaped but do not permit the water to escape and consequently warp and crack. The third property is density and power to vitrify under heat. *Clays* must have a refractory nature, so that they do not collapse or fuse during the firing, but all will depend upon the degree of heat to which the clay is subjected.

Most English earthenware bodies are compositions of ball clay from Devon and Dorset, china clay or kaolin from Cornwall, calcined flint stones from the seashores, and Cornish stone. Each of these ingredients is balanced one against the other. Ball clay to give plasticity, china clay to give whiteness and strength. Flint and Cornish stone to give porosity, strength, and fire resisting qualities. In commercial pottery-making as many different recipes are used as there are potteries, and the various types of pottery all call for different compositions, making definition a highly complicated affair.

A further complication occurs when glazes are used, as these have to fit the body. A mutual relationship must exist between the body and glaze used, otherwise many faults, crazing, crawling, etc., may result. It will be readily understood that from the various materials, and by a correct adjustment of the ingredients, a body can be composed to suit the requirements of the worker in any type of pottery-making.

Unless one is prepared to compound one's own body from the natural minerals however (which is a tedious, complicated and messy business), it is better after trial and error, to purchase prepared bodies from a regular source. For Schools and Institutions, this is by far the best course to pursue, as the preparation of the body (unless one is fortunate in having a local clay which requires but little attention and additions) requires much equipment and many hours of labour. If a local clay is used, all factors of heat, glaze, decoration, must be fitted to it, thus imposing strict limits. The one limit to which most workers and students will wish to confine themselves will be the limitation of firing, by the degrees of heat attainable by the particular kiln they happen to possess.

Strictly speaking, types of pottery can broadly divide into three classes.

Earthenware, stoneware and *porcelain,* each having a different body and each bearing qualities of a different nature, yet each having its own particular æsthetic appeal.

Earthenware is pottery, whether glazed or unglazed, which is porous in the biscuit state after being fired. It is sometimes called *faience,* and is always opaque. In texture it may be coarse or fine, and it may be white or coloured. For hygienic purposes, it needs completely glazing with a non-crazing glaze, otherwise particles of food, dirt, etc., are absorbed into the porous biscuit. Various types of glazes are used on it which may be either transparent or opaque. These are alkaline in nature, such as Persian Faience, lead glaze, boracic glaze, or glazes rendered opaque by the use of tin and other opacifying agents.

Stoneware, differs from earthenware, by being vitreous in nature, and differs from porcelain by being non-translucent. It is really a kind of earthenware burned at a greater heat. It is, therefore, as its name implies, much stronger. Natural clays are sometimes used if they do not lose their shape when fired to vitrification, or by overheating.

A mixture of fireclay with a more fusible clay, or even felspar may be used. It is often glazed with *salt glaze,* but when this is unsuitable, the body may be fired to the biscuit state and glazed with similar glazes used for earthenware. It is also often softly baked (900° centigrade) to facilitate handling and then coated with a glaze that matures at the same heat as the body. As the latter must be vitrified, a less fusible glaze must be used which generally means a leadless glaze.

Porcelains differ from other kinds of pottery in being translucent. They are also hard and vitreous. No single natural clay will give porcelain, and the mixtures are often less plastic than earthenware or stoneware bodies, making the technique more difficult. True porcelains are made of white burning materials, though there are many mixtures used for making the various kinds. They are briefly called *hard paste* and *soft paste* porcelains ; the terms refer to the relative hardness or softness of the fired paste, but more so to the refractory nature of the bodies. The *soft paste* porcelains are more like opaque glasses. The true *hard paste* of the Chinese is a mixture of kaolin and petunze. Our English version of porcelain has a large percentage of bone ash in its composition, hence the term *bone china.*

Points to remember about bodies:—
All clays and bodies contract when drying and firing.
Earthenwares about one-tenth to one-twelfth.
Stoneware about one-ninth to one-tenth.
Porcelain one-fifth to one-eighth.
All can be rendered into slip by the addition of water, but slip will have more contraction that the plastic body.

Dry body can only be brought back to the plastic state by being thoroughly kneaded and wedged, after the correct amount of water has been added.

The various materials from which bodies are made differ greatly according to the source from which they are obtained, but the ceramic chemist has done much to balance mixtures to serve the particular requirements of the ceramic medium.

The ancient potter had to rely on local sources of clay, and in doing so a particular type of pottery was produced. Ancient Egyptian potters simply used Nile mud mixed with sand; likewise the Persians used a body composed mainly of sand with a little clay added to hold it together : such a body would have but little plasticity and would consequently be difficult to throw.

Red clay or terracotta. The peasant potters of England mainly used red clays which have the necessary plasticity and contain a high percentage of iron. These red clays can be found in many localities and fire at a comparatively low temperature on account of the iron content. They formed the basis of English slipwares ; chiefly made prior to the eighteenth century and are used nowadays for the so-called common red teapots, floor tiles, plant pots, etc. Artist potters find these clays suitable for their uses ; when decorated with slips and other various treatments.

Ball clay. Found in Devon and Dorset and mined by excavation. They are sometimes known as blue ball clays or black ball clays. All varieties are plastic and after firing the biscuit is usually a strong cream colour. Used alone they are too plastic, do not dry well, contract too much and warp, but they form the basis of white earthenwares and are most valuable as an admixture to other bodies ; providing very often the necessary plasticity.

China clay or kaolin, Has very little plasticity and consequently often requires the addition of a more plastic clay such as ball clay to make it workable. It is white and is decomposed granite. It forms the basis of porcelain and is used in earthenware bodies ; being low in contraction and high in porosity it casts quickly. In England it is mined in Cornwall and it is won from the parent rock by washing and levigation. Other deposits occur in China, France, Germany and the U.S.A.

Fireclays are plastic ; refractory to heat and fire to a buff colour. Their chief uses are for the making of refractory articles such as crucibles, furnace linings, etc., and can be used by the artist potter as the basis of stoneware bodies. They are found in various parts of the Midlands, Wales and the North country and some of them are found underlying the coal measures.

The following tables are intended to give some idea of the composition of various bodies :—

Red body	Red clay	... 60
	China clay	... 30
	Flint ...	... 10

White Earthenware	Ball clay	... 25
	China clay	... 25
	Flint ...	... 35
	Stone...	... 15

Bone China body	China clay	... 25
	Cornish stone	25
	Calcined bones	50

Felspathic Porcelain	China clay	... 50
	Felspar	... 25
	Quartz	... 25

Red body	Red clay	... 85
	Fireclay	... 15

White Earthenware Lime body	Ball clay	... 48
	China clay	... 12
	Flint ...	... 34
	Whiting	... 6

Bone China body	China clay	... 24
	Cornish stone	28
	Calcined bones	48

Stoneware body	Buff fireclay	... 50
	Ball clay	... 20
	Flint ...	... 15
	Felspar	... 15

II. Built-up shapes

Coiling, pinching and slab-built-pieces. Given good plastic clay, the fingers can fashion shapes of varying size and form. Where no wheel is available, round shapes can be made by coiling and pinching; square shapes by building with thin slabs of clay. For the school, these are excellent methods to start with, in fact it is exactly how primitive man must have begun his early pot making.

Coiling. The clay, after being kneaded or wedged, is rolled out on a wet plaster slab (or smooth board with a non-sticky surface) into long ropes of clay about three-eighths of an inch thick, or more, according to the size of the pot to be made (*Fig.* 1). The base may be made from

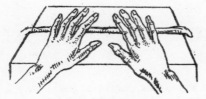

Fig. 2. *The base for a coiled pot.*

Fig. 1. *Rolling the clay.*

a flat coil of clay or from a flat disc of clay (*Fig.* 2). The walls are raised by coiling the ropes one on top of the other, round and round, each ring being carefully welded to the lower on the inside as the wall progresses (*Figs.* 3-4). Outward bulges are achieved by building outwards a little,

Fig. 4. *Welding the inside of a coiled pot.*

Fig. 3. *Raising the wall of a coiled pot.*

and incurves, vice versa. The outer surface of the pots may be smoothed over, or the coils may be tooled together in a decorative pattern, but a coiled pot will never have the concentric look of a thrown pot and should be treated accordingly. Handles made from rolls of clay may be added, stuck on with a little slip and welded on to the pot (*Fig.* 5). When really

Fig. 5. *Surface treatment for a coiled pot, with handle fitted.*

large pots are to be made, of a size which cannot be made on a wheel, coiling is perhaps the most feasible manner of making them. It is really surprising how symmetrical a well-made coiled pot can be. Coiled ware is made by the natives of South America, Uganda and New Guinea, and is practised as a handicraft in our primary and secondary schools.

Pinched pottery. This is similar to coiling, except that the walls are built by pressing small pieces of clay around the edges of the base forming a smooth ring which is kept vertical by means of the hands. The process is continued until the required height and shape have been attained. The surface is finished by rubbing and scraping. This is again an excellent way of making really large pots, and it is the method by which the large refractory glasshouse pots are made for the glass industry. The natives of Tanganyika and other African tribes make fine symmetrical shapes by this method with only the aid of a beater to consolidate the clay and an old crock to scrape the sides.

Slab-built pieces. By rolling out thin slabs of clay into various shapes and bending them while still moist, interesting forms can be made (*Fig.* 6). Or the slabs can be left to harden a little and cut up into pieces to be stuck together with slip ; rather like joinery is done. By this method, all sorts of square and oblong shapes can be made. On the occasion of the birth of a child to the peasant potters of Staffordshire, a miniature cradle would be made in this manner and the name of the child and the date of its birth would be trailed in slips upon it. Money boxes in the form of cottages are excellent examples for schools, thus combining pottery with some knowledge of architecture. Whatever form is attempted, the various pieces must be well joined with slip and the inside corners welded together and strengthened with rolls of clay firmly modelled into the shape (*Fig. 7*). It must be remembered in this case that once clay

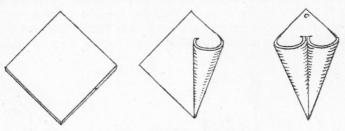

Fig. 6. A wall-vase for flowers.
(*a*) the flat slab of clay.   (*c*) second corner rolled over and
(*b*) first corner rolled over.   fastened down.

has hardened, it has lost its plasticity and cannot be bent. These various primitive ways of making pottery shapes are of excellent educational value in schools.

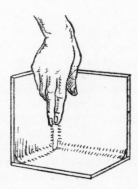

Fig. 7. Slab - built
pottery: fastening
the sides together.

Pinched, coiled and built-up figurines, animals. In all ages and periods ; for as long as pottery has been made, potters have made for amusement or for more serious reasons, small figures, animals, birds, etc., either singly or in groups. Some were used for religious rites, or as burial effigies, many as toys for children and others for purely decorative purposes. It is quite a natural action to take a piece of clay and squeeze and pinch it into shapes, letting one's fancy and imagination have free play. Examples of this kind of work can be seen in the pottery statuettes of ancient Egypt, in the tomb figures of the Chinese, the bird whistles of ancient Mexico and Peru, and in the early Staffordshire chimney ornaments, indeed wherever clay was used ceramic art was produced, possibly as recreation from the more mundane task of producing pots of a utilitarian nature.

The plastic nature of clay and its ability to retain any form it is modelled into, together with the hardening by heat makes all this possible. It is an easy transition from pinched, coiled and slab-built pots to applying the same principles to small sculptures. As hollow pots are usually reasonably thin and are relative to the size and speed of the kiln in firing, burst pots due to imprisoned air and steam are not often experienced, but with the thicker and more solid models certain precautions must be taken and

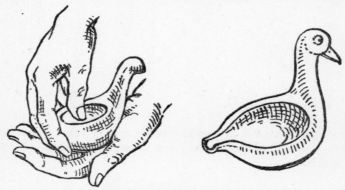

Fig. 8. The pinching method started from a ball of clay.

modelling methods understood before work commences. It may well be argued that bricks and tiles are solid ceramic material, but bricks and other large objects of clay are heated very slowly ; days of drying and firing take place as against hours in the case of pottery. It therefore follows that kilns and firing cycles must be related to the size and solidity of models and, of course, the nature of the clay used whether coarse and sandy or smooth and close grained. The finer the material the thinner must be the walls, and some system must be followed of putting the work together in order to avoid it being ruined by bursting in the kiln. Everything will depend on the subject matter, quality of clay and size. Most earthenware bodies can have walls, rolls and balls of about half an inch thickness, and fire, after being well dried, without much trouble. Exercises using pinching, rolls, balls and slabs could be made, followed by combinations of all methods. In fact, there seems no limit to skill and ingenuity, combined with imagination, but the best work æsthetically is often that which follows the simple technique. One important rule must be followed when one piece of clay is fastened to another : the two pieces of clay must be smeared at the joint with a little thick slip and then the two pieces pressed gently together and afterwards well modelled into each other with a finger or modelling tool until all traces of the joint are obliterated (*see Fig.* 9). Care must also be taken to see that the various pieces such as limbs or heads are of about the same condition, as a wet piece stuck on to a dry piece will contract unequally, resulting in cracks, or a rupture of the pieces. It is also extremely difficult to fasten dried clay pieces together, because when clay is dry it loses its plasticity and adhesive powers and the process of modelling together cannot be done. See plates II to V and XXII, XXIII.

Fig. 9. Making a joint.
Make a puddle of slip. Brush a little on to the joints. Press and model together.

Dishes, trays, made with the use of simple moulds. From flat pancakes of clay which may be rolled out by means of a rolling pin and board (in the manner of rolling out pastry) all sorts of symmetrical and asymmetrical shaped dishes can be easily made with the aid of a simple mould to give shape to the clay and to support it during the drying period.

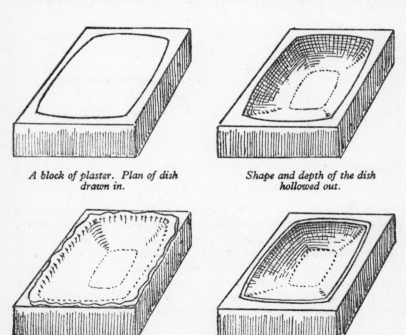

A block of plaster. Plan of dish drawn in.

Shape and depth of the dish hollowed out.

A pancake of clay laid in the mould.

The top edge trimmed and interior smoothed.

Fig. 10. The hollow mould.

Moulds are dealt with in a subsequent chapter, but the most simple form of mould, a depression in a block of plaster, requires but little skill to achieve. Fill a cardboard box of the required length, breadth and depth with plaster, pouring in the mixture of plaster and water while still fluid so that it will find its own level. For this purpose the plaster should not be mixed too hard, an approximate mixture of 1 measure of water to 1¼ measures of plaster would do. These quantities might vary for different grades of plaster.

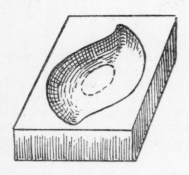

A block of clay or plaster with shape hollowed out.

After sizing: Filled with plaster and stalk built on.

The mould withdrawn from the model.

A pancake of clay laid on, trimmed and smoothed.

Fig. 11. The humped mould.

After the plaster has set the cardboard walls can be removed and the plan of the dish can be drawn on the top level surface of the block of plaster. The curves and depth of the dish can then be scooped out with scrapers and finished with glass paper. The mould should then be allowed to dry thoroughly. When this has been done a pancake of clay of the appropriate size and thickness can be made. If this is rolled out on a board a thin cloth of muslin or other absorbent material should be stretched across the board to prevent the clay from sticking to the board. Peel the clay from the board and place it face down into the mould, exactly in the manner of putting pastry into a pie dish; tearing away the cloth before the clay is gently patted and smoothed into firm contact with the shape of the mould with a damp sponge. The surplus clay at the top can then be removed with a knife or wire stretched between a prong, and the whole of the interior smoothed with a potters' kidney-shaped rubber. The dry plaster will speedily absorb the moisture from the clay dish, which after a while will shrink away from the mould and the dish can then be easily tipped out of the mould on to a level board (*see Fig.* 10).

It is a simple transition from the hollow mould to one which gives a reverse impression, that is a humped mould, sometimes called a ' mushroom mould.' Scoop out a piece of clay or plaster the required shape, then mix and pour plaster into this concavity and also build up a stalk on to what will be a mushroom shape when taken away from the model. Again dry the plaster mould and the pancake of clay is then placed on the top of this form, the mould in this case forming the interior of the dish, the exterior being smoothed in the manner of the preceding method, and the overlapping edges also cut back level to the edge of the mould. It must be pointed out that in this case the clay will contract on to the mould somewhat, so that the sides and angles should not be too steep, otherwise some difficulty may be experienced in removing the clay dish from the mould intact (*see Fig.* 11, *plates VI to IX*).

III. Throwing and turning

The *throwing* wheel is the most ancient of all the potters' machines. It has largely been superseded by the *jolley* which is really only a more mechanical form of throwing machine, but is still the most æsthetic way of making a piece of pottery. Fortunately its decline has been arrested by the revival of the potters' craft in studio and school, where it is the principal method of forming shapes other than flat pieces like plates and dishes. In the factory it is usual to find throwing used only for the production of ' art ' pieces and other forms, such as large electrical insulators, etc., for which it is still the best possible way of making.

A thrown pot has individuality which a more mechanically made piece can never have, and it is in this direction that its future lies.

In principle *throwing* consists of shaping a mass of clay on a revolving horizontal disc. The mass is centred by pressure of the hands—after which the clay is pulled up into a hollow form and shaped by pressure of the hands from within and without into the desired form (*Fig.* 12). In practice it requires the most correct manipulation to deal with the centrifugal action of the spinning wheel and keep the pot concentric, but by careful practice and by doing the correct movements at the right time and by applying the correct speed, most people can learn this most fascinating art. It is somewhat difficult to give written or illustrated

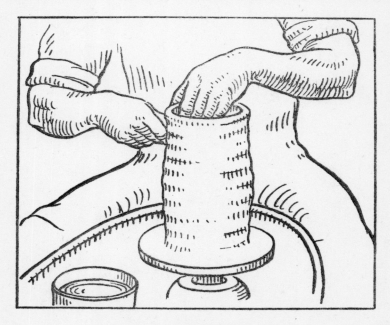

Fig. 12. *Throwing a pot.*

instruction, as a practical demonstration or motion picture is needed to give the correct co-ordination of hand movements and speed, but if careful consideration is given to the following and if it is mentally recorded before attempting to use the wheel then some success should be achieved.

Wheels. There are many types of throwing wheels, but the principle of a revolving disc on a vertical spindle remains the same—only the motive power is different. Wheels are either driven by kicking a heavy fly-wheel at the base of the spindle, or propelled by a kick bar coupled to a crank above the fly-wheel; or the spindle is driven by a rope from a large gear wheel. The latest modern types are electrically driven (*Figs.* 13-15).

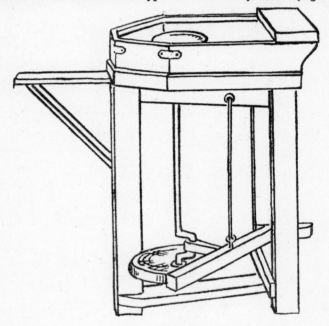

Fig. 13. A kick wheel.

The preparation of the clay for throwing is of the utmost importance. It must be perfectly homogeneous and without air pockets and also of the right consistency of dampness. If very wet and soft, it will not stand up, but will squat upon the wheel; if too hard it will make the throwing laborious. Much will depend on the nature of the shapes to be made. Large pots require a stiffer clay, small ones can be made with a softer clay. To work the clay before throwing, it must either be put through a pug-mill, which is like a huge mincing machine (*see plate I*), or be kneaded and wedged by hand.

Wedging. The clay in a goodly quantity (about 10 to 20 lbs.), is put upon a block of damp plaster, stone, cement, or wood—anything with

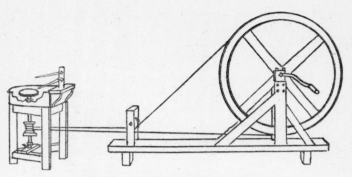

Fig. 14. *A rope-driven throwing wheel.*

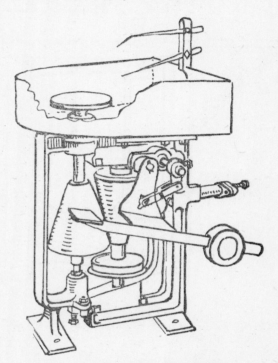

Fig. 15. *A power-driven throwing wheel.*

a firm clean surface will do, not too porous or smooth, otherwise the clay will stick, although this may be overcome by stretching a canvas type of cloth across it. The mass is cut in two by a brass wire, the top half reversed and raised above the head and brought down smartly, smacking and spreading the lower half on the block. Turn the whole lump about and keep repeating the process as many times as are necessary in order to make it homogeneous. It must be remembered that if two very flat surfaces are brought together, a loud bang will ensue and air may be imprisoned in the clay, hence the need for reversing the top half over, thus presenting a rounded side to the under flat surface (*Fig.* 16). Kneading is a rotary movement having a similar effect. Wedging and kneading are laborious but absolutely essential, as time and energy spent on getting the clay into condition will save many heartbreaks when actual throwing takes place.

Fig. 16. *Wedging the clay.*

Throwing. The clay is made into balls as round as possible, about 2 lb. per ball is a good size to start with. (Later, when larger pots are attempted, it is better to shape the clay into cones.) The ball is then thrown on to the disc by the right hand, being guided on by the left. Setting the wheel in an anti-clockwise motion and basting the clay with water, the left hand is pressed against the revolving clay, forcing it to the centre. The elbows should be tucked well into the sides or rested on the edges of the throwing box and both hands brought into play with a pincer movement (*Fig.* 17). The whole of the left hand should be around the ball and the right-hand fingers around the left, allowing a sliding movement.

Fig. 17. *Centering the clay by coning.*

Fig. 18. *Depressing the clay cone.*

21

Then the ball is shaped into a cone by squeezing the palms of the hands towards the centre of the ball. The pressure should be nearly across the diameter. This forces the clay upwards and if the hands are inclined inwards with pressure at the right place, the result will be a centred cone. Squeezing may take place as the hands move downwards from the top of the cone, thus further extruding the cone upwards. Any wobble is thus worked out at the top.

To depress the cone (*Fig.* 18) place the ball of the left hand (the metacarpal bone of the thumb) on the top of the cone and press downwards, keeping the fingers around the sides and the arm quite steady. Any effect of mushrooming of the mass can be counteracted by lateral pressure with the right hand. It cannot be emphasized too greatly that

Fig. 19. *Opening the mass.*

Fig. 20. *First movement to raise the wall.*

it is the left hand and arm which do most of the work at this stage and it is good practice to try this centring with the left hand only. Repeat this movement until you have a perfectly centred squat cylinder. To open this upwards and outwards (*Fig.* 19), keep the hands cupped around the cylinder and insert the right thumb dead in the middle (both thumbs can be used on a larger mass of clay) and push the thumb downwards and then slightly outwards, leaving sufficient clay to form the thickness of the base. Then, keeping the right thumb inside, turn the right-hand fingers underneath the hand and grasp the left wrist with them, thus bringing the two wrists together (*Fig.* 20); this enables you to squeeze the thumb backwards and towards you, at the same time pulling up the thinning wall. A tendency of the wall to spread outwards should be countered by pressing the left hand inwards.

At the end of this movement, both hands are taken from the top of what should be the start of the hollow cylinder. The final thinning is done by inserting the left hand vertically into the inside of the cylinder to support it, while pressing and lifting against the outside with a bent index finger of the right hand (*Fig.* 21). The wall is thinned in this movement by starting at the base and slowly bringing the hands upwards. It may take repeated actions of the movement to accomplish this. The co-ordination of speed and hand-movement is important.

For the centring of the ball plenty of speed is necessary, up to 900 revs. per minute, but for the opening and thinning, 100 revs. per minute, while for tall pots at the finish 50 or 60 revs. are fast enough. When the cylinder has been duly thinned, it may be shaped by pressure from within and without by various movements of the hands, pressing out a bulge from inside the pot or bringing in the top (*Fig.* 22). All this time the clay must be kept wet with frequent bastings at the start of each movement.

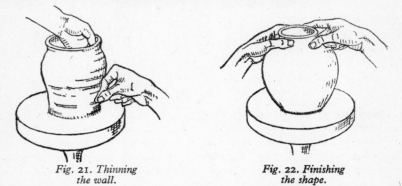

Fig. 21. *Thinning the wall.*   Fig. 22. *Finishing the shape.*

The chief fault in throwing is wobble ; this is caused either by unsteady hands and arms, or by unequal squeezing. Any eccentricity can only be worked out at the top where it can be cut off by a needle or piece of wire pulled taut between the thumbs. If narrow-necked pots are required, the cylinder should be kept narrow at the top right from the start, for it is extremely difficult to decrease a wide-mouthed opening, as the centrifugal action of the wheel tends to widen the mouth. To counteract this, it is good practice to leave a somewhat thicker ring at the top of the cylinder. For the same reason bowls are easy to throw provided that too flat a section is not attempted.

Fig. 23. *Cutting the pot off the wheel.*

To cut the pot off the wheel, clean away the surplus clay from the base with a turning tool, and then with the wire pulled taut and pressed down on to the wheel by the thumbs, swiftly cut it clean off the wheel (*Fig.* 23). If a little water has been splashed on to the wheel head, the pot may slide off easily with a little push at the base and be gathered into the hands, but care must be taken not to distort the soft shape. If it is a jug which is being thrown, the spout may be bent outwards at this stage, by bending the lip forwards with the left index finger, whilst supporting the rim with the thumb and forefinger of the right hand (*Fig.* 24). The pot may be left to dry a little if it is very soft, but the spout must be formed before the clay has lost its plasticity.

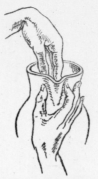

Fig. 24. *Shaping the spout of a jug.*

Bowls are difficult to cut off, owing to their width. They are best made on separate plaster slabs fastened down on to the wheel head and removed completely with the bowl made on it, leaving the cutting off until the body has hardened a little. Lids are usually thrown upside down leaving plenty of clay at the base in order to produce the knob by turning (*Fig. 25*).

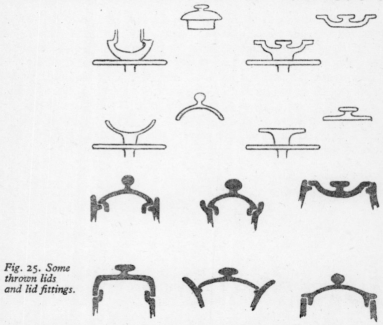

Fig. 25. *Some thrown lids and lid fittings.*

Spouts can be produced from narrow tapering cylinders; cut and shaped when harder (*Fig. 26*).

Fig. 26. *Thrown spouts.*

A few important points for beginners to remember about throwing:—

(1) See that the clay is in the right condition.

(2) Make the ball or cone really round.

(3) Throw it dead in the centre of the wheel.

(4) Present a stiff and steady left arm with the elbow well tucked inwards towards your body.

(5) Keep the clay well basted with water.

(6) Adjust the speed of the wheel to the varying needs in accordance with the progress of the pot.

(7) Do not attempt too large a pot to begin with.

(8) Never snatch the hands away from the shape.

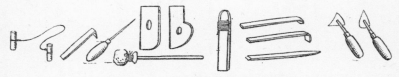

Fig. 27. Some throwing and turning tools.

Turning. After the shapes have been dried into a semi-hard condition —resembling firm cheese—they may be finished on a horizontal lathe (*Fig.* 29), or inverted on the throwing wheel (*Fig.* 30). If a pot has been well and truly thrown, it should require but little turning, but the base

Fig. 28. Some thrown shapes:
(*a*) *Mycenaean, in the author's possession.*
(*b*) *Coffee pot by the author.*
(*c*) *Teapot by the author.*

will probably need some attention (*Fig.* 28). Turning is precisely similar to the corresponding process used for shaping wood, metal, etc. The shape must be centred and fastened on to the lathe, whether vertical or horizontal, by means of a little clay or by welding the pot on to a *chuck* which is a round block of wood screwed on to the spindle. Hollow *chums* may be used for narrow-necked articles, into which the pot is inserted. The body should be cut, not scraped, and the tool held firmly to prevent

it vibrating. Some form of hand rest should be provided for steadiness'
a slide-rest in the case of the horizontal lathe (*Fig.* 29), and a long stick

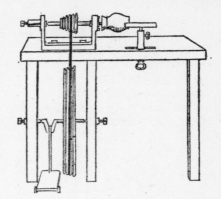

Fig. 29. *Turning on
a treadle lathe.*

in the case of the vertical method (*Fig.* 30). Turning tools can be made
from pieces of iron hooping, bent, shaped and filed with a keen edge
(*Fig.* 27). Turning should be done with great restraint and only where
necessary, otherwise the pot will lose much of its character (*Fig.* 31).

Fig. 30. *Turning on the wheel.*

) ( ) ( )) ( ) (

〰 〰 〰 〰 *Fig. 31. Some lips and feet.*

Handles and spouts. It is at this stage after turning, that handles and spouts are attached. The clay must not be harder than the firm cheese state, for if it has lost too much of its plasticity, adhesion of the separate pieces will not take place. The handles and spouts, as far as is possible, should be of the same state of hardness and contraction, otherwise tensions will be set up when the pieces are stuck, due to unequal shrinkage.

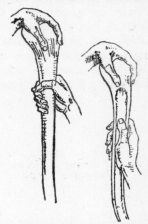

Figs. 32-33 ' Pulling ' handles.

They may be attached with a little slip (clay and water) and firmly welded together to make the separate parts into one whole, otherwise there may be a tendency to spring and crack away. Handles may be *pulled* from a conical mass of clay held firmly in the left hand and extruded downwards. This gives a gently tapering, natural handle form (*Figs. 32-33*). The clay requires basting with water as in throwing. After being *pulled*, the handles require hanging up to dry a little, after which they may be cut and bent to the required length and shape. Excellent handles of uniform thickness and of any length and section, may be cut by means of wire loops. In this case, the wire loop is dragged through a mass of homogeneous clay, cutting and pulling with it, a strip of clay of the section of the wire loop (*Fig. 34*). This strip is then bent to the desired shape, dried a little and then attached to the pot.

Wheel-made or thrown sculptures. The artist-potter and particularly the sculptor will quickly see the possibilities of forms and shapes thrown on the wheel ; composed and assembled together to make hollow (and therefore easily fired) sculptures. In this case the vision of the potter must be of fundamental and basic forms and in creative design, reducing natural

27

forms to great simplicity, yet retaining in a subtle way that which differentiates the good form from the bad. It is trite to say that a good shape needs no decoration, but it is also nevertheless true. Very often a beautiful shape which may be useless for any practical purpose is good sculpture and a piece of decoration in itself. All pots do not have to be made to hold flowers or as vessels for food and drink, but in themselves, may be, works of art. It is in this category that wheel-made sculptures fall; as also would coiled and pinched sculptures as well as moulded forms.

The potter may find it necessary at first to draw his ideas on paper and to follow up this first conception by accurately throwing the necessary pieces at one and the same time. All that remains to do is to allow the various component parts to harden and then to cut and fit together, fastening the pieces with slip and modelling the joints firmly together, taking care to leave holes connecting the pieces together for the free passage of air and steam during firing. It follows too that the various methods of decorating may be indulged in; slips, scratching, colour, and also glazing if required (*see plates XVIII to XXI*).

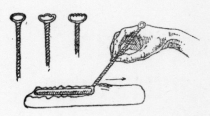

Fig. 34.
Cutting handles by means of wire loops.

IV. Moulds for pottery making

Knowledge of mouldmaking is necessary for the modeller, as the two go hand in hand. The modeller must consider the number of parts his model will require when being moulded. Simple shapes, such as saucers and plates are of course reproduced from single moulds, as are most cups and bowls if they are fundamentally wedge-shaped, not incurved or with feet incurved. If the model is to be reproduced on the jolley, it must be perfectly round and true ; if for casting a little irregularity does not matter much, but even so, it is better perfectly accurate.

Early moulds appear to have been of wood, metal or alabaster. The ancient Greeks and Romans, and in some cases Early Staffordshire potters, used fired clay (or biscuit) moulds. Between 1743 and 1750 Ralph Daniel of Cobridge, introduced from France the use of plaster moulds.

Plaster of Paris (calcium sulphate) is produced by heating or ' boiling ' gypsum or plaster stone. It is made by heating the stone to a temperature of about 160°F. when it appears to ' boil ' It is then removed, cooled and sifted. If it is overboiled it swells too much and does not mix well ; if underboiled it will not set properly.

Moulds of plaster are now generally used for the manufacture of pottery because they are easily and cheaply made, and because they are highly absorbent—drawing the moisture out of the clay rapidly, so permitting the pressed or cast shape to be delivered quickly. They may also be reproduced with ease and this is important, as they wear out after a few dozen pieces have been made. Any number of moulds can be produced from the original mould.

Moulds of wood are used for articles of very simple shape, such as bricks and crucibles, etc., and moulds of baked clay are sometimes used instead of plaster moulds. These latter are sharp and clean and more durable, but are more expensive and only slightly absorbent, and so have a lower output than moulds of plaster.

Moulds of baked clay are preferable for the reproduction of applied ornament such as leaves, low-relief figures and similar. The clay is pressed into the mould, and the surplus scraped off with a knife before removing the ornament from it (*Fig.* 57). Plaster would not stand up to such treatment. Moulds of brimstone (sulphur) are sometimes used for this purpose of ornamenting as they are easily made and are harder than plaster. They are oiled before use to prevent the clay " squeezes ' from sticking.

The Model. For reproduction by jolleying or by casting and pressing, an exact model of the intended article has first of all to be made. This model is usually in clay or plaster, but other materials can be used. If produced in clay it is usually solid, but sometimes is built up on a plaster core. This core helps to prevent the clay from twisting.

When modelling, allowance must be made for the contraction of the body during firing; the model must be made bigger than the actual finished piece will be (for contractions, see page 8).

The tools required for modelling and turning models are:—

Turning tools of all shapes and sizes for shaving down.

Metal scrapers (spring steel) with straight edges and toothed for extra scraping.

Steel spatulas and toothed tools of a variety of shapes.

Wooden modelling tools, various shapes.

Measuring instruments, rulers, set squares, compasses, dividers, etc.

Sponges, brushes—stiff hog's hair and soft sables.

Polishing horn or thin spring steel.

The clay used for the actual modelling of the model should be a good quality modelling clay free from grog. Irregular shapes, such as figures and animals, are modelled straight-forwardly from soft clay and allowed to harden a little before moulding. Round models can be lathe-turned, either vertical or horizontal, though handles, spouts, etc., are modelled separately. For either shapes it may be best to prepare a block of soft clay a few days before it is required, so that it may have time to stiffen a little. Very simple circular shapes, such as saucers, plates, dishes and similar, are turned directly from plaster on the vertical wheel (usually a hand jigger) and the upper surface only is produced (the *under* surface is usually made by a metal tool on the jolley).

The *jigger*, which is a belt-driven whirler, is a necessary piece of equipment in the modeller's and potter's workroom. It is extensively used by modellers, mouldmakers and pressers, and consists of a thick plaster disc which revolves on a spindle. It is usually supplied with just a pronged head on to which one runs the plaster disc. Its many uses make it virtually the potter's bench (*Fig.* 35).

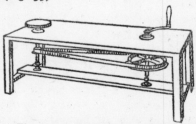

Fig. 35. *A mould-makers' 'jigger.'*

Note on mixing plaster. The plaster should be of superfine quality. Do not use building plaster as it is too coarse. It is sprinkled into water in the proportions of about one and a half to two pounds of plaster to one pint of water. After the powder has soaked for a minute it is stirred fairly vigorously for a few seconds, and then poured on to the model, after which it is allowed to set hard for about twenty minutes. It is most important to have the right mixing of powder and water. If insufficient powder is added the result will be a soft mould; if too much is added the mould will be too hard and will not be sufficiently absorbent. Various grades of plaster differ considerably, but usually the above proportions will be about right. It is equally important to mix the plaster fully, and not to pour it on to the model too soon of too late. It should be just on the change; just as soon as it begins to thicken perceptibly.

Sizing. When one plaster impression is taken from another the latter must be soaked in water for a few minutes if it has become dry, and then treated with diluted soap (usually soft soap) to kill the porosity and to stop the two from sticking together. The size (or diluted soap) is made by dissolving soap in hot water to the consistency of syrup or thin oil. The plaster shape is then lathered with this solution, using a soft sponge or brush. This is then washed off with clean water. The process is repeated at least three times, but at the last lathering it is not washed off but wiped clean with a soapy sponge, removing all bubbles of soap, but leaving the surface slightly greasy. All this has worked up a face on the plaster, so that the slightly fatty surface will enable the impression taken from it to be delivered freely. This sizing or lathering, must be done every time one impression is taken from another.

Fig. 36. *Making a mould for a cup, for ' jolley.'*
(a) *Making the mould.*
(b) *The plaster turned to fit the jolley head.*
(c) *Section of finished mould.*

The Moulds. As all moulds wear out in time, it is necessary, when a large number of identical articles have to be made, to have a permanent model or mould from which other moulds can be reproduced. This master-mould is called the *block* which is the original mould made from the model. From this block mould a reverse impression is taken, giving back the form of the model; this is called the *case*. From this case mould, an unlimited number of working moulds can be made simply by casting impressions. If the case gets damaged or broken, another one is made from the block, which is always retained for this purpose only.

The several processes of making pottery requiring plaster moulds, are *casting*, *pressing*, *jiggering* and *jolleying*. For these purposes, the moulds have a slightly different function. In some cases the mould makes only one surface of the ware, as in jolleying and pressing, but in some casting processes the moulds form all the surfaces.

Making a set of moulds for a cup and saucer. To make a set of moulds for a cup and saucer to be made on the jolley, the models are first prepared by turning out of hard clay or plaster. The handle is modelled separately from stiff clay. The cup model is centred on a circular plaster slab on a jigger or whirler, sized, and a wall of linoleum is tied around the base slab (*Fig.* 36). The plaster is poured in and before it has set hard the lino wall is removed and the mould is turned to fit the tapered head of the jolley. When the model is removed from this *block* mould, a *case* is taken from which the required number of working moulds are made. The saucer follows the same procedure (*Fig.* 37). Both are one-piece moulds, as the moulds in these cases make but one

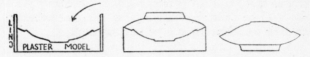

Fig. 37. *Making a mould for a saucer, for ' jolley.'*

surface and the tool of the jolley the other surface. The handle is different ; it will be made in a two-piece mould by pressing. Half of the handle is buried in soft clay while an impression is taken of the other half (*Fig.* 38).

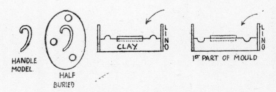

HANDLE MODEL. HALF BURIED CLAY 1ˢᵗ PART OF MOULD

Fig. 38. *Making a mould for a handle.*

When this has been done, the whole is turned over, and the clay removed so that the second half may be made. Keyways must be sunk in order to key the two sections of mould together. These are made by boring little hollow hemispheres into the first half, so that when the second half is taken, they will appear as humped impressions which fit the moulds exactly together.

THE TWO PARTS OF THE MOULD WITH GROOVE FOR SURPLUS CLAY.

Fig. 39.

To facilitate the pressing of the handles, a groove is cut into both halves of the mould close to the handle, to receive the surplus clay squeezed into it (*Fig.* 39). In the making of all plaster moulds which are in more than one piece, all surfaces not being taken in the particular impression must be buried. Linoleum or stiff paper walls for curved surfaces and wooden boards for flat surfaces are erected and securely bound with cord to hold the plaster while setting. In this way moulds having any number of parts can be made. Handles and spouts are not always separated, but are sometimes incorporated into the complete mould.

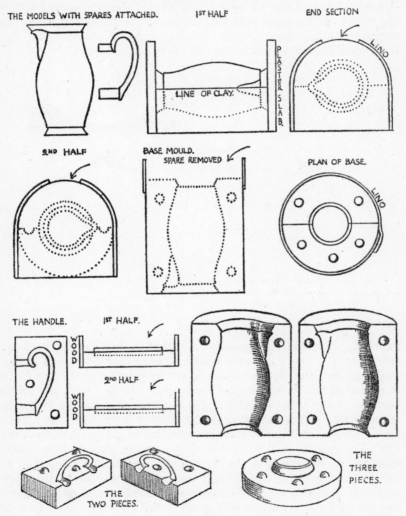

Fig. 40. *Making a complete mould for a jug, for the casting process.*

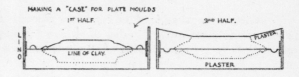

Fig. 41. Making a 'case' for plate moulds to be reproduced.

Other moulds. Moulds are of greater service in making forms which cannot be made on the wheel, such as square shapes, figures, etc. When both surfaces are to be made by the mould, only one surface is modelled. From this the first half of the mould is made and on this, a pancake of clay is laid to give the thickness of the article ; then the second half of the mould can be made, with the necessary arrangement of a hole for casting. If a dish mould for the pressing process is required, only one surface will be necessary as in the case of the jolleyed wares.

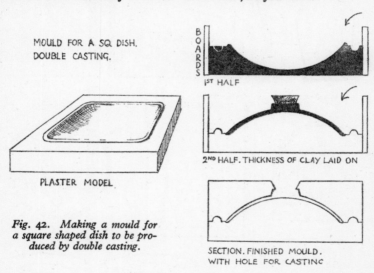

MOULD FOR A SQ. DISH.
DOUBLE CASTING.

PLASTER MODEL.

Fig. 42. Making a mould for a square shaped dish to be produced by double casting.

1ST HALF

2ND HALF. THICKNESS OF CLAY LAID ON

SECTION. FINISHED MOULD.
WITH HOLE FOR CASTING

Pressing. In this method pancakes of clay of the required thickness are pressed onto or into the plaster moulds. In the case of a mould in one piece such as a dish, the pancake is spread by knocking it out on a block of plaster similar to the wedging block, with a *batter*. This is a round block of plaster with a slightly convex surface about seven inches in diameter mounted on a handle, usually made of pottery (*Fig.* 44). Both must be soaked in water to prevent absorbtion of the moisture from the clay. The pancake of clay is polished by means of a special long palette knife and is then placed on to the mould, a wet sponge being used to dab the clay into close contact with the surface of the latter. It is then smoothed over with a kidney-shaped piece of flat rubber and the spare clay cut off the edges with a long needle called an *etchel*. If a foot is to be raised on the dish, it may be built up by means of another mould

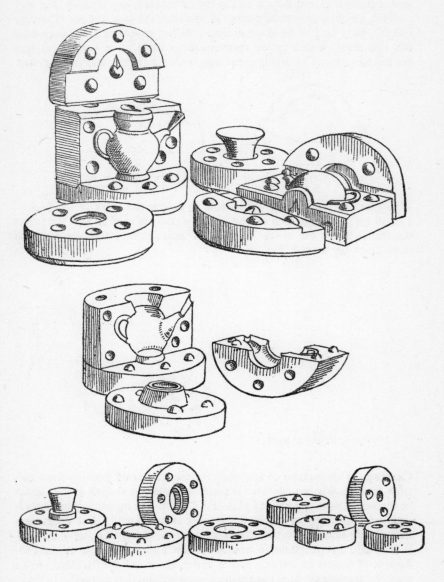

Fig. 43. *A complete 'case' and working moulds, for a teapot.*

with a suitable groove placed on the top of the clay, and filled in (*Fig.* 45).

If the mould is in several pieces (as would be the case of a jug or similar object), each part is filled separately and the mould is then assembled and tied firmly with a strong cord or leather strap. The various sections are joined together by welding the clay with the fingers and rolls of clay.

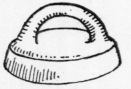

Fig. 44. *A presser's 'batter.'*

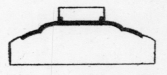

Fig. 45. *Section of a pressed* **dish**, *with foot.*

If the neck of the piece is too narrow to permit the entry of the fingers, a small bit of sponge, tied on the end of a stick, is used to join the seams together. When the article has dried a little, it may then be removed easily from the mould (*Fig.* 46).

Fig. 46.
The ' presser ' at work.

Casting. This method of shaping ceramic articles by pouring fluid clay (*slip*) into moulds is a convenient method of making shapes which cannot be thrown or wheel-made (*see plate XXIX*). In the industry it has largely replaced ' pressing,' as it does not require so much skill. The craftsmanship mainly falls on the mouldmaker in the provision of suitable moulds. It is chiefly advantageous in producing cast figure work and in the production of shapes in ceramic bodies which are insufficiently plastic to be made on the wheel. It is essentially a mass-production method. In principle it is very simple ; the dry plaster mould absorbs the moisture from the slip, leaving a deposit of firm clay on the surface of the mould. When this deposit is thick enough, the remaining slip is poured away, leaving the hollow cast which, after drying a while, is removed by taking the mould, or parts of the mould, from it. Its chief defect lies in the fact that when the mould has a number of parts to it, seam marks are unavoidable. These have to be scraped away or *fettled* with a knife, and sponged over. Nevertheless they often show after firing. Pressed articles have the same defect.

Making the slip. Good casting slip cannot be made merely by adding water to the clay; this contracts far too much, due to the large amount of water necessary. Sodium silicate and sodium carbonate are added to give fluidity—thus cutting down the amount of water required, but if added in excess, will cause a flux on the biscuit-ware, which does not then take the glaze properly. Sodium silicate, when added to the extent of 0·25 per cent reduces the viscosity of a slip weighing 36 ounces to a pint, to that of an untreated slip weighing about 26 ounces per pint. Rather more sodium carbonate is required in the proportion of about four of carbonate to three of silicate. At factories, slip is made in large quantities by means of *blungers* which churn the clay, water and soda into the fluid state. A small amount can be conveniently made in a bucket, by shredding the clay, pouring over it the soda dissolved in hot water, and allowing to stand for a day, after which it may be stirred by hand, and passed through a suitable sieve ready for use. Some 25 lbs. of clay make a good bucketful. The amount of silicate of soda required for this would be about one ounce and the carbonate of soda about one and a third ounces, dissolved in about one quart of hot water. The amounts would vary for different bodies, and more or less water can be added according to the needs.

The first casts made from plaster moulds are usually ' wasters ' as there is generally a scum on the surface of the moulds from the mould-making process. After the first few casts, the moulds deliver the casts more freely.

Casting moulds require ' spares ' to allow for the sinking of the slip. These can be trimmed off in the fettling and finishing, after the cast has been removed from the mould ; or they can be cut away previously.

POTTERY SCULPTURE

Reproducing figures, animals, etc. The reproduction of small sculptures in ceramic bodies follows a similar course to that pursued for the reproduction of plaster casts from piece-moulds*, except that the figures are often cut into many pieces by severing heads, limbs, etc., and making separate moulds of these. This facilitates the making of the figure either by the casting or pressing processes. They are afterwards assembled by sticking each separate part in its right place with the aid of a little slip and the joints carefully modelled over.

A solid model is first prepared in clay, preferably without armature, as this interferes with the cutting up of the figure, and with due allowance for shrinkage in the fire. Care should be exercised in the design of figures for reproduction with due regard for the material involved, as

* See *Plaster Casting* by V. Wager. (Alec Tiranti.)

Fig. 47. *A model of a figure cut up ready for moulding, and the manner of burying half of the model in clay.*

unbalanced figures, and figures balanced on toes, would be difficult to keep upright in the fire and would emerge drunken or mis-shapen. Often, difficult poses have to be propped during drying and firing, to keep them from falling out of shape. Also, extended or protruding limbs or other parts, are easily damaged, for although pottery is one of the most lasting of materials it is easily broken by a fall or blow.

(1) **Moulding.** The figure model when completed, should be well planned for the moulding, the necessary parts severed, and a faint line drawn on the parts indicating where the seams will be. It is often better to cut the figure into many parts rather than attempt to keep it in one or two pieces, for the ensuing clay cast will shrink a little before it can be taken from the mould, and parts which lock or bind-in will crack. In principle each separate limb, etc., should deliver from a two- or three-piece mould, and have no undercuts or large projections.

When starting to mould the pieces, it is better to attend to the heads and limbs first, laying them down on a board in a bed of clay, and burying the under-half up to the seam mark. If a large model, protect the un-covered part with a layer of tissue paper while preparing the job. Work the fence or wall at right angles to the model as far as possible, and to ensure a faint seam mark, lay the clay as sharply as can be to the mark, with a steel spatula. The bed of clay should be wide enough to allow ample space for notches or joggles, and its shape, square or oblong in

38

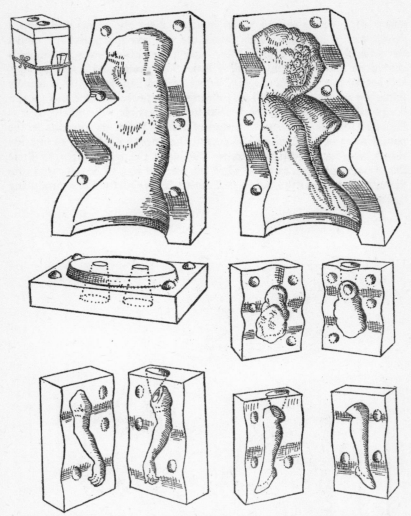

Fig. 48. Various sections of the finished moulds and the manner of tying the mould with cord.

accordance with the shape of the model. Walls of wood, clay, or other material are then erected around the whole, and tied firmly with cord to contain the plaster which is poured in. After about twenty minutes, this will have set and the walls can be removed, the job turned over, and the clay fence taken away, exposing the cast edges. These plaster edges thus exposed are sized with the solution of soft soap and water as in other forms of moulding, the walls set up again, and the second half poured in. All the pieces are done in the same way, whether planned for two, three or more pieces, and when completed, they are opened by means of a wedge-shaped knife, inserted along the seams and tapped gently with a hammer. This forces the sections apart, and the model can then be removed easily. After cutting the casting holes, the moulds should be cleansed lightly with a little clean water and a soft sponge, and set aside to dry thoroughly, before casting can begin. It is usually necessary to dry the moulds in a drying atmosphere of some sort ; a few hours in a gas oven with the heat as low as possible will suffice. If it is intended to press the copies instead of casting them, the opening in the mould must be large enough to permit the finger to reach in to join the seams together. V-shaped grooves cut along the seams often facilitate the pressing process, as these allow the surplus clay to be squeezed into them, but casting is the easiest and most effective method of reproducing figure work.

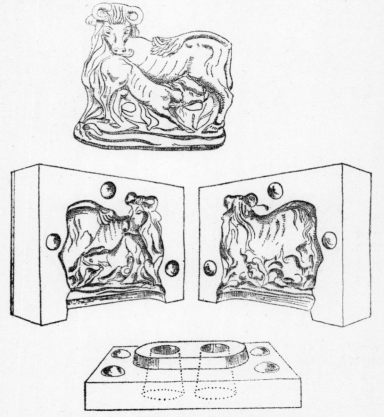

Fig. 49. An animal group and its three-piece mould.

(2) **Casting.** When the moulds are dry, they are tied with cord, and the slip is poured in ; this should be kept level with the top of the mould

by repeated fillings, as the slip sinks down. After a correct thickness of clay has formed on the surface of the plaster, about one-eighth inch or more, according to the size of the model, the remainder is drained out and the cast allowed to stiffen for a little while, after which it may be easily removed by opening the mould. It should be remembered that the first, and sometimes the second or third casts out of a mould, are often wasters, as they are inclined to stick a little until the surface of the plaster has been cleaned by the slip.

(3) **Repairing.** When the separate parts are all cast, they must be assembled before the clay dries. The spaces created by the casting holes and the seam marks, are trimmed with a sharp knife and brushed lightly with a soft brush or a fine sponge. Where a head or limb is attached to a body, or other part, a hole must be cut to permit a continual passage of air, as imprisoned air is likely to cause a burst or crack during firing, owing to the imprisoned steam which may be generated. A little slip applied to the joints, together with careful modelling and repairing of the joints and seams, finishes the piece which must then be slowly and carefully dried ready for the firing.

(4) **Reproducing the moulds.** The life of the mould, like all plaster moulds for pottery, is limited to some 50 or 100 copies, but if more are required, the moulds may be reproduced by *cases*, or a master-model of plaster, lead, or other material can be kept, from which further moulds can be made when necessary.

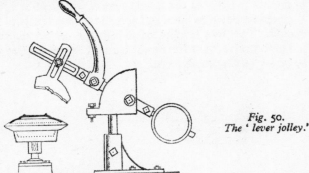

Fig. 50.
The ' lever jolley.'

Jolleying. This is really a mechanical form of throwing. Although less skilful than hand-throwing, it requires some skill to work the machines as no machine has yet been invented in which clay can be fed to emerge a pot at the other end. It is a mass-production method by which large quantities of cups, saucers and plates can be made of uniform size and shape. The *jolley* machine for plates, usually consists of two machines working together ; the *spreader* which flattens out balls of clay into pan-cakes rather thicker than the article is required to be, and the *jigger* part of the machine. This is a revolving head (shaped like a plant-pot) into

41

which the mould is placed. It has a pull-down lever to which is attached the tool—a profile shape of the back of the plate (*see Fig. 50 and plates XXV and XXVI*).

Fig. 51. The ' vertical jolley.'

To make the plate, the pancake of clay is placed on the mould which has the form of the top surface of the plate in reverse. The mould is then placed on the head of the machine and, while it is revolving, the operator presses the clay to the mould with a wet hand or sponge. The tool is then drawn down to press and spread the clay firmly to the surface of the mould. This tool is adjusted to give the correct thickness to the plate, and to form its foot or rim on the base. The surplus clay is trimmed from the edges with a needle etchel.

Fig. 52. The eccentric movement of the tool of the ' vertical jolley.'

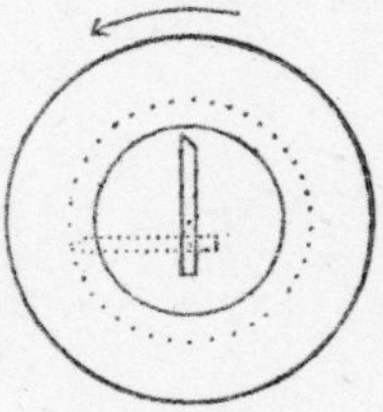

Cups and hollow vessels follow the same procedure, except that a ball of clay is fed into the hollow cup mould and is thrown roughly up the side of the mould. Then the tool descends to finish off this throwing process ; the surplus again being cut off with the etchel.

The action in both these cases, take but a part of a minute, and in this manner, the machines, assisted by the operators, turn out cups, saucers and plates in the four figures in the course of a day.

The moulds, when filled, are put into a drying chamber where the articles dry gradually and evenly.

Jolleys are of two types—the *lever jolley* and the *vertical jolley*. The latter enables shapes with distinct bulges to be made, for, as the tool descends into the shape, it is pressed against the side by means of an eccentric twist. A twist back again enables it to be withdrawn easily (*Figs.* 51-52).

Special jolley machines make elliptical dishes. In this case, the tool is again stationary and the mould on the head of the machine moves around it, in an eccentric motion.

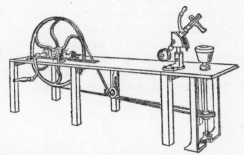

Fig. 53. *A rope-driven 'jigger' and 'lever jolley.*

V. Tiles

Tile-making forms an interesting department of ceramics, and has an extensive historical background. Glazed tiles are made chiefly for wall surfaces, and unglazed tiles for paving. Ceramic mosaics which are tiny cubes of pottery material, also form interesting patterns when the tesseræ are used to form the design.

There are two principal methods of making tiles—the plastic method and the dust-pressed. In the former, which would be the one used in educational institutions, the clay is either pressed into wooden or plaster moulds of varying size and thickness, or cut by means of wire into the thickness and shape required, from a block of clay. The chief difficulty in the making of these plastic tiles is the buckling during drying. All flat pieces of moist clay tend to curl at the edges as these dry first and tensions are set up owing to this unequal rate of shrinkage. This may be overcome by careful stacking and drying (*Fig.* 54).

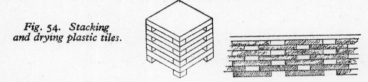

Fig. 54. Stacking and drying plastic tiles.

The clay used for tile-making need not be so plastic as that required for throwing; in fact it is far better to add grog (previously fired clay crushed and ground) to it. This prevents buckling to a great degree during drying and firing; as much as one part of grog to two parts of clay can be used. Good tiles can easily be made a dozen at a time by constructing a rough frame on a stout board and filling this with the mixture of clay and grog (*Fig.* 55). Allowance must be made for the

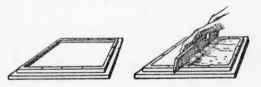

Fig. 55. A simple frame for making twelve tiles at each filling.

contraction of the body due to drying and firing, which might be about one-twelfth, varying according to the body used. The depth of the frame should be according to the thickness required. Plastic-made tiles measuring six inches square would need to be about half an inch thick. The surface of the wood should be dusted with a little fine grog powder to prevent sticking and the clay pressed into it firmly to avoid air-pockets, and afterwards levelled and scraped flat and smooth by means of a straight wooden or metal scraper.

The tiles may then be cut with a sharp knife and ruler. If marks are put on to the frame, this will save measuring each time the frame is filled. After drying a little, the tiles are easily turned out of the frame for stacking and drying. Plaster moulds to make a single tile may be made and filled in a similar manner. If the moulds are reproduced by the 'Case' method, many tiles can be made at the same time. Plastic-made tiles can be decorated by all the various processes of pottery decoration, slips, inlaying, underglaze painting, or enamels, at the respective stages of production.

In the industry, from which is demanded accuracy of size and shape, tiles are made chiefly by the dust process. In this case, the clay is partly dried and crushed into a fine powder. This is fed into the steel well or 'box' of the powerful press and a heavy steel die descends into it, forcing the dust against the die at the bottom of the box. The pressure is so great that the dust is compressed into a solid of the required size and shape. The pressure makes them strong enough to be ejected from the box and to be handled and fettled with safety. The 'green' tiles as they are called are thus practically dry and are ready for firing, thus avoiding the buckling during drying (*Fig.* 56). Mosaics are made in a similar manner.

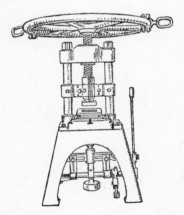

Fig. 56. *A screw press for the production of dust-pressed tiles.*

Raised line tiles. This may be produced either with a tube line tracer as in trailing slip on to pots, or by means of a line sunk into the plaster mould. The raised line on the tile acts as a dam for the coloured glazes which are filled into the interstices, like the Spanish tiles of the fifteenth century.

Stoneware tiles. By using a coarse stoneware body, excellent tiles for fireplaces and stoves can be made by hand, and glazed with stoneware glazes. These tiles have more beautiful colourings than the ordinary commercial tiles and stand up to heats much better. An excellent body for this purpose is the T material supplied by Coupe, Tidman Ltd.,

Pontypridd, or any mixture of fireclay. This can be made into small tiles, blocks or briquettes made from plaster moulds. When blocks are made, the hollow interiors should be strengthened with buttresses of clay to keep them straight and even, during firing. In the trade, these blocks are known as *faience* and are used for exterior as well as interior work. The glazing of tiles is chiefly executed by dipping the surface of the tile into the liquid glaze. This is speedy and efficient, but not fast enough for the industry where, in some cases, the tiles pass on a conveyor belt underneath a ' waterfall ' of glaze in a quick and continuous movement.

VI. Decorating processes

Many and varied are the processes by which pottery and porcelain can be decorated. Almost every technique of the painter and *décorateur*, both flat and in relief, has been exploited. Reproductive methods of printing in monochrome and polychrome have been used, and the range of the colour palette is nearly unlimited. One important factor stands out—that all the colours used in ceramics must be derived from the metals in order to withstand the heat necessary for the baking of the ware.

Our museums provide a fount of inspiration, from the primitive scratched line and earthy pigments, to the wonderful enamels of the Chinese. Outstanding, will be found the exquisite blue-tinted glaze of the Egyptian and Persian potter, the red and black of the Greeks, the marvellous lustres of the Persian and the Hispano-Moresque styles, the amazing arabesques of the Italians, wonderful monochrome glazes of the Chinese, and hosts of others right down to the present day.

Classification is difficult, for pottery can be, and is, decorated at any of its stages of production; in the clay state, on the biscuit, on and in the glaze. For colouring, much depends on the temperatures at which the wares are fired, for some metallic oxides burn away to a greater degree than others. It may well be that a piece of pottery, having nobility of form and beautiful glaze, will need no additional decoration, and the artist would not attempt it. For similar reasons a pot should be conceived at the start as a whole, and not have decoration applied as a means of hiding its defects. Prepared colours for the various processes can be purchased from the specialist suppliers.

DECORATION IN THE CLAY STATE

The incised line. While the clay is still fairly soft, lines are drawn in with a sharpened wooden tool, and stains rubbed into them. The lines keep the colour in place even though it may be a volatile stain. The English *scratch blue* salt-glazed wares were produced in this manner as also were many of the German grey stonewares. The Chinese, in the Sung dynasty, used carved lines in conjunction with the lovely celadon glazes on porcelain. In this case, no colour was rubbed in, but the glaze filled-in the lines to a greater depth and so registered a darker tint.

In the Middle Ages, the monks produced encaustic tiles by carving the clay tiles to a good depth and filling in the pattern with a different coloured slip. The pattern, being inlaid, still remained even when the tile was partly worn; through being used for the paving of the Abbeys and Cathedrals.

Raised decoration. Many styles of pottery have been decorated with reliefs; notably the German stonewares, the products of the Elers Brothers,

47

and the Jasper ware of Wedgwood. This method has something of the nature of sculpture and sometimes when the relief is high it interferes with the line of the pot.

The relief modelling is first produced and then a mould is made from it. This may be of plaster, unglazed pottery or brimstone. The pottery ones wear the best, and are sufficiently porous to permit fairly rapid delivery of the clay which is pressed into it, scraped level, and lifted out with a steel spatula. These reliefs are then stuck on to the damp clay pot with a little slip or water (*Fig.* 57). Different coloured bodies may be used to

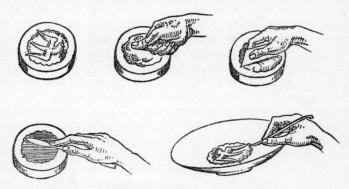

Fig. 57. *Raised modelled decorations: taking a pressing from a mould and applying it to a pot.*

heighten the effect. The brimstone moulds, which also wear well, are made by melting sulphur in an oven and pouring it on to the model. After cooling, it may be used, but it requires oiling to prevent the body from sticking to it. The Elers Brothers used brass dies and stamped a small lump of clay on to their pots.

Slip decoration. Trailing. This is perhaps the most natural way of decorating in the clay state. The slip in this case being a natural clay, is diluted with water until it is like a fluid batter, and then passed through a 60s mesh sieve. It may be white, or coloured with oxides or the prepared

Fig. 58. *A glass syringe, and rubber bag with a glass nozzle for slip decoration*

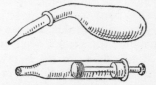

body stains, according to the tint required. There are several ways of using the slip. It may be poured or trailed on to the pot in the manner that icing is applied to cakes. A rubber bag is filled by means of a glass syringe and a glass or plastic nozzle is inserted into the mouth of the bag (*Fig.* 58). When held in the hand and squeezed gently, the slip will emerge like toothpaste from a tube, and swiftly drawn raised lines of slip can be thus produced upon the pot. Most of the English slip decorated wares of Wrotham and Staffordshire were produced in this manner, except that a small pottery vessel held the slip and a quill or hollow reed was inserted to regulate the flow. Decoration applied in this manner should be liberal and luscious, as the slip loses height when dry, and looks poor if not applied thickly (*Fig.* 59).

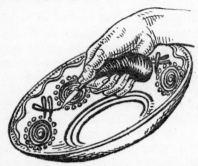

Fig. 59. Applying slip decoration with rubber bag and glass nozzle.

Marbling and combing, etc. As these effects are difficult to produce on veritcal surfaces, it is easier to start with flat pancakes of clay upon boards. To *marble*, a coating of slip is poured upon the clay, levelled and drained off, but before it is dry, other coloured slips are trailed into it. These do not mix but when the boards are shaken and twisted violently they mingle into most intricate marbled patterns.

To effect *combed patterns*, trail lines of coloured slips across the wet coating of slip and then draw a long thin pointed instrument (a fine brush will do) across the lines in one or both directions. It should make no line itself but drag out into the background the coloured line in most beautiful feathered effects. After the pancakes of clay have stiffened, they can be made into shapes by pressing them on to, and into, moulds. After practice, it is possible to do marbling and combing on upright shapes. In these methods, chance plays an important part and repetition is out of the question. In fact, it is purely a matter of dexterous trickery. A further method of using slip is on the *sgraffito* principle. A pot, when in the cheese-hard state, may be dipped into a different coloured slip and this, when hardened, may be scratched or drawn through, revealing the background. The background can be used to make the pattern, or vice versa.

Slips may also be used for painted patterns, but they do not lend themselves readily to this treatment. In every case care should be taken to ensure adhesion of the slip to the body of the pot. It is good practice to sponge the surface of the pot before applying the slip. This roughens it a little and makes a better contact. Slip cannot be applied to clay which has dried beyond the cheese-hard state, as it will not adhere but crack off, owing to the unequal contraction of the two. The amount of body stain to be mixed with the slip varies according to the tint required ; from five per cent to twenty per cent of stain can be used. After firing into biscuit, the whole can be finished with coloured glazes if required.

DECORATION APPLIED AT THE BISCUIT STAGE

Underglaze painting. This is by far the best method of painting on pottery, for the colours being applied on to the biscuit are then covered with a transparent glaze which gives them a pellucid quality unobtainable by the technique of painting on top of the glaze. In some cases the colours swim upwards into the glaze and in others, the colours being volatile, give a softened flowing effect. The range is quite extensive, and they may be purchased, prepared and ground, ready for use. The browns, blacks, yellows, oranges and yellow greens, do not flow, but the blues from the cobalt, purples, blue-greens and greys readily expand. Pinks, crimsons and delicate matt blues are obtainable, but it must be remembered that when using underglaze colours on different bodies and with different glaze compositions, the colours are liable to produce different tints accordingly. It is therefore advisable, when using them with different types of ware, to test them thoroughly.

A range of colours can be tested on one piece of pottery, which can then be kept as a future guide for that particular body and glaze. The colours stand temperatures from 950° to 1150° centigrade, and a more limited range of colours can be obtained for use on porcelains at 1300° centigrade. The technique is fairly simple ; the colours are ground on a glass slab or tile with a palette knife, using water with a tiny drop of gum arabic* which will fix the colour on the biscuit, and prevent rubbing or smudging when the glaze is applied ; it is then painted directly on to the ware. Some of the colours change during the firing ; thus, some blues, from cobalt, may appear as a black powder, but emerge from the glaze firing an intense blue. Some practice is needed in order to judge the thickness of application as some are more powerful stains than others, but experience will give the relative strengths. Colours from cobalt and copper are the most powerful ceramic stains, and should therefore be used with great restraint.

In factory practice, it is usual to use a medium of turpentine and fat oil† for painting, as this gives greater manipulation of the colours. The

---

* A little dextrine or treacle added to the water gives the same result. Glycerine added to the water gives a better painting medium. If too much medium is used it causes the colour to flake off before firing.

† Fat oil may be made by filling a tea-cup about three parts with best turpentine slopping a little over into the saucer and putting them in a warm place. The turpentine will travel up the inside of the cup and down the outside, into the saucer. As this action goes on, the spirit of the turpentine evaporates and fat oil is produced in the saucer.

colours are ground on the tile with turpentine, and a few drops of fat oil are added to help the colours to flow evenly from the brush. Sable tracers are the best for outlining, and camel-hair brushes of different shapes, both rounded and chisel-ends, can be used for filling in the outlines, or putting on washes (*Fig.* 60). For running on lines and bands

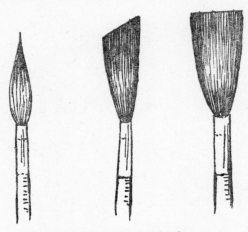

Fig. 60. *A pottery painter's brushes.*
(*a*) *Tracer.* (*b*) *Liner.* (*c*) *Bander.*

of colour a wheel is necessary. The article is centred upon the wheel, and the brush, charged with colour, is held on to the revolving article. Centring requires some practice, and is most easily performed by placing the article on to the wheel as near the centre as possible, setting the wheel in motion and then tapping the article, as it revolves, into the centre (*Fig.* 61). A hand-rest is necessary to keep the hand steady when applying the line or band; a small stick is useful, or the wrist may be rested on the bench, if the wheel is below the level of it.

When turpentine and fat oil are used as a medium, the painted ware must be fired at a low temperature (about 700° centigrade) in order to burn out the oil and fix the colour, to enable the ware to be glazed; for the glaze would not take on the oily surface.

Underglaze printing from copper plates. This method of ceramic decoration, which has been in use for some 200 years, is used extensively by pottery manufacturers. Most people will be familiar with that hardy perennial of pottery decoration, the *willow pattern* in cobalt blue. Although this method bears a strong relationship to engraved book illustration from which it originated, it is, nevertheless, capable of a treatment entirely of its own (*see plates XL and XLI*). The principle difference in technique between engraved book decoration and that for pottery, is that in the case of the pottery technique, a transfer is made upon tissue-paper, so that the copper plate does not come into contact with the ware. In detail, the method is as follows.

ENGRAVING. The design is first produced on paper and is then engraved upon a copper plate of about one-eighth of an inch in thickness. The design may be traced upon the copper; not in reverse, but in the way

Fig. 61. Running bands and lines on a plate with the aid of the lining wheel.

in which it is to appear on the pottery. In factory practice, much of the labour of tracing has been eliminated by the application of photography. If the design has to fit a concave or convex surface, allowance must be made. To do this the engraver lays tiny bits of wax over the part to be printed, and then presses upon this a piece of tissue-paper, thus taking an impression. The wrinkles are smoothed out and the gores marked or cut out. Then the paper impression is removed and laid flat upon the copper, giving the required form. In the actual engraving, the lines are cut much deeper than for bookwork. This is of the utmost importance, as the colour used will contain about one-third of thick oil, which will be burnt away later, in the firing. V-shaped gravers of varying angles are used for the lines, and punches producing dots or clusters of dots to give graded tints. Both hatching and cross-hatching may also be utilised. For some colours, particularly reds, a much stronger line is needed, but a shallower line may be used for enamel colour printing on top of the glaze as this is not subjected to the intense heat of the glost fire, but to that of the enamel fire, which has a much lower temperature.

PRINTING. Upon the engraving being accomplished, the transfer is taken on a sheet of fine pottery tissue-paper which is saturated by being brushed with a solution of soft soap (about an ounce to one pint of hot water to dissolve it); this will enable the paper to be peeled away from the colour after its transfer to the ware.

To effect the transfer, a hot stove is needed and a powerful press

(*Fig.* 62). For schools, the etching equipment can be used. First, the colour is mixed upon a hot iron slab or bakestone, with a palette knife. About two parts of colour to one of special printers' oil (for biscuit ware). This is a mixture of linseed oil, red lead, resin, etc., but it can be bought ready for use from potter's suppliers. The copper plate is placed on the

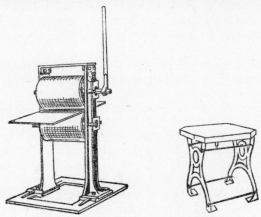

Fig. 62. *The printer's press and hot stove.*

hot stove and the mixed colour rubbed into the engraved lines by means of a wooden dabber with a convex surface, so as not to scratch the copper (*Fig.* 63*a*). The reason for the heat is to make the thick oil work more easily ; the object of this will be apparent later, when the transfer is used on the ware. After being worked into all the lines of the engraving, the surplus colour is scraped off by means of a steel or wooden spatula

Fig. 63. *A printer's tools.*
(*a*) *The dabber.*   (*c*) *Corduroy boss.*
(*b*) *Steel spatula.*   (*d*) *Roll of flannel.*

with a flat chisel end (*Fig.* 63*b*). This does not completely clean the surface, which is then bossed clean by means of a pad covered with corduroy (*Fig.* 63*c*). (For taking a few prints, I have used a rubber squeegee very effectively for cleaning the copper.) The plate being duly inked, it is then laid upon the bed of the press and the saturated tissue-paper laid upon it, covered with a printer's blanket as in taking a proof of an etching) and passed through the press. The saturated paper is thus forced into direct contact with the colour in the engraving. The copper plate, together with the tissue paper on it, is then placed on the hot stove and as the copper plate becomes warm again, the paper is carefully peeled off, carrying with it the impression in colour of the engraved pattern.

For the rapid production of printed transfers, the factories use a machine into which is built an engraved roller. Colour is fed into the engraved lines of the roller, which is cleaned automatically. The printed transfers emerge on a continuous band of tissue-paper, and are cut off as required.

TRANSFERRING THE PATTERN TO THE WARE. The tissue-paper will have dried by the action of the heat, and it is then trimmed of unnecessary paper with scissors and pressed face down upon the surface of the biscuit ware. It is further forced into strong contact with the ware by means of a bound roll of flannel (*Fig.* 63*d*), using the end of it, which is lubricated with soap ; or an extremely stiff type of stencil brush, likewise lubricated, may be used. After rubbing the print firmly and evenly and without disturbing the paper, the ware is then immersed in cold water when the tissue-paper will float away, leaving the pattern on the ware. The object of the stiff oil is now apparent ; were the oil and colour soft enough to be used cold, it would not resist the action of the water or the cold surface of the biscuit ware, but as it needed heat to make it workable, the cold water and cold surface of the ware cause it to harden at once, and leave it unharmed. The printed ware then requires firing at a low temperature (about 700° centigrade) in order to fix the colour and burn out the oil so that it may be glazed, as the unfired glaze, being suspended in water, would not take on the oily surface. This is known as the hardening-on fire.

VII. Glazes and glazing

As nearly all ceramic articles are of two distinct materials—clay for the body of the pot, and glass (called glaze) for its outer covering—no one at all interested in the production of any type of pottery or porcelain, can ignore this important latter branch of the craft. The scientific mind will find immense interest and a fascinating subject with a wide field for experimental work ; the artist, great satisfaction and delight in the control of this part of the work, which enables him to clothe his forms, to enhance their beauty, to give them protection and to make them more serviceable. The finest work in this respect has been produced by artists with a scientific bent, although much has been done by technicians putting their more intimate knowledge at the service of the creative artist.

Glazes can be defined as any impervious glassy materials used to cover or line a ceramic article in order to prevent it from absorbing liquids, to make it more hygienic, to beautify it, and as a protection or foundation for various kinds of decoration. They are very closely related to ordinary glass, as both consist of mixtures of various silicates in solid solution, and both have a fusion range and not a sharp melting point. Ceramic glazes must always consist of mixed silicates, or silicates and borates, and not be a single definite compound as this would eventually become crystalline, instead of remaining glassy. Glazes also differ from glass in containing a larger proportion of alumina. They are usually broadly classified into lead and leadless glazes, and can be further classified as either raw or fritted.

Application of glazes. Glazes may be applied in various ways ; by dipping the ware into the mixture, by spraying, pouring or painting. Dipping or spraying is the simplest and best way of getting a level and even coating on the ware, but large pieces can be painted quite easily if a small quantity of gelatine or gum is added to the glaze ; the required thickness of the coat can be built up by several applications. This is the manner in which large pieces of sanitary wares are glazed.

Preparation of glazes. The preparation of glazes is well within the scope even of the amateur, for, given but a slight knowledge of chemistry, suitable glazes can be compounded to fit the various types of natural clay or body. The necessary materials to do this may all be procured easily, ready ground, and in any quantity.

Unless the materials are purchased ready ground for use, they must be ground to a finely divided state, either wet or dry, through a ball mill or other grinding apparatus (*Figs.* 68 and 69). The various ground materials are then weighed out in their proportions, mixed with water to the right consistency, and passed through a sieve of at least a 120 mesh

(*Fig.* 70). The consistency of the glaze will depend on the porosity of the biscuit ware to be glazed.

Raw glazes and calculations. Raw glazes consist of materials which are insoluble in water and are merely ground to a fine powder and mixed in their correct proportions with water. Certain clays, loams, etc., are of such a composition that they may be used, without any addition, as natural glazes, but they are rare and only suitable for coarse wares.

Fig. 64. Glazing the inside of a pot by swilling.

Fig. 65. Glazing the outside of a pot by pouring while revolving the pot on a turntable.

Fig. 66. Spraying glaze. The glass hood and revolving fan to take away the laden atmosphere.

Fig. 67. Dipping plates into glaze by means of three claws tied onto the thumb and fingers.

Glazes are expressed in the form of molecular formulae, percentage composition, and by the actual working recipes. Recipes are almost worthless unless one can translate them into molecular formulae, because a given recipe must be adapted to the different conditions created by the use of different clays and bodies, the source of the different materials, and even the change of firing conditions. One cannot know too much about the chemical composition of the materials being used, so that every effort should be made to understand as much as possible about the ingredients used and their chemical actions under heat.

Fig. 68. A porcelain jar
mill for grinding glazes.

Fig. 69.   Mixing and
gringing glaze with a
pestle and mortar.

From the molecular formula of a glaze it is possible to foretell its physical characteristics with some degree of probability. This would be extremely difficult with either the corresponding recipe, or percentage chemical composition, unless translated back into molecular formula. These formulae are of the greatest value in restricting the field of experiment and where changes of glaze composition have to be made.

Fig. 70.
Sieving glaze.

In order to use formulae, one needs to use the chemists' form of shorthand, in which each element is represented by the first letter of its Latin name, or by two letters, when one is not convenient. In such a manner

H is the letter representing hydrogen, the lightest of the elements with the atomic weight of 1 ; Pb are the letters representing lead (the Latin name is Plumbum) with the atomic weight 207·2, as 1 atom of lead is 207·2 times heavier that 1 atom of hydrogen. When a substance is a compound of two or more elements it is represented by the appropriate letters, called symbols, following each other. Thus PbO represents a compound of lead and oxygen, with a molecular weight of 223·2 which is, of course, the combined weight of the lead and oxygen added together. When the symbol is followed by a small figure it means that the atomic weight of the symbol letter must be multiplied by the number following. Thus Al_2O_3 means Al atomic weight $27 \times 2 = 54$; O, atomic weight $16 \times 3 = 48$. The combined weight of the two elements in their respective proportions therefore is $54 + 48 = 102$, the molecular or combined weight of alumina. From this it can be seen that the formula of a chemical compound is a shorthand method of writing down the proportions of the different elements forming the compound. Where the symbol is preceded by a figure on the same line as in $2,Al_2O_3$ it means that there are two units of the compound equalling, in this case, the number of 204. Thus the formula for clay represented by $Al_2O_3.2SiO_2.2H_2O$ has the molecular weight of 258 ; Al_2O_3 being 102, $SiO_2 \times 2 = 120$, $H_2O \times 2 = 36$, total 258.

Table of the atomic weights of the elements used in ceramics.

Element	Symbol	Atomic weight	Element	Symbol	Atomic weight
Aluminium	Al	27·0	Manganese	Mn	55·0
Antimony	Sb	121·7	Mercury	Hg	200·6
Arsenic	As	75·0	Molybdenum	Mo	96·0
Barium	Ba	137·4	Nickel	Ni	58·7
Bismuth	Bi	209·0	Nitrogen	N	14·0
Boron	B	11·0	Oxygen	O	16·0
Bromine	Br	80·0	Phosphorus	P	31·0
Cadmium	Cd	112·4	Platinum	Pt	195·2
Calcium	Ca	40·0	Potassium	K	39·0
Carbon	C	12·0	Selenium	Se	79·0
Chlorine	Cl	35·5	Silicon	Si	28·1
Chromium	Cr	52·0	Silver	Ag	108·0
Cobalt	Co	59·0	Sodium	Na	23·0
Copper	Cu	63·6	Strontium	Sr	87·6
Fluorine	F	19·0	Sulphur	S	32·0
Gold	Au	197·0	Tellurium	Te	127·6
Hydrogen	H	1·0	Tin	Sn	119·0
Iridium	Ir	193·0	Titanium	Ti	48·0
Iron	Fe	56·0	Uranium	U	238·0
Lead	Pb	207·2	Zinc	Zn	65·4
Lithium	Li	6·9	Zirconium	Zr	91·2
Magnesium	Mg	24·3			

Table of pottery compounds, minerals, etc.

	Symbol	Molecular Weight	Remarks	Fusing Point
Alumina	Al_2O_3	102	Is a constituent of clays.	
Antimony oxide	Sb_2O_3	288		
Albite (soda felspar)	$Na_2O. Al_2O_3. 6SiO_2$	526		1200°
Alkalis			See potassium oxide and sodium oxide.	
Anorthite (lime falspar)	$CaO. Al_2O_3. 2SiO_2$	278·6		
Antimoniate of lead			Gives yellows.	
Barium carbonate	$BaCO_3$	197	Basic.	
Barytes (barium sulphate)	$BaSO_4$	229	Basic.	1500°
Boric acid	H_3BO_3	62		
Borax (sodium viborate)	$Na_2B_4O_7. 10H_2O$	382	Supplies both acid and base to soft glazes.	
Calcite (calcium carbonate)	$CaCO_2$	100	Marble. Whiting. Chalk. Basic substance for glazes.	
Carbon dioxide	CO_2	44	Poisonous.	
Chromium sesquioxide	Cr_2O_3	152		
Cobaltous oxide	CoO	75	Gives blues.	1500°
Copper oxide (cupric black)	CuO	79·6	Gives greens and turquoise. If reduced, red.	1080°
Copper oxide (cuprous red)	Cu_2O	143		
Copper carbonate	$CuCO_3$	124	Used for reduction.	
China clay	$Al_2O_3. 2 SiO_2. 2H_2O$	258		
Cornish stone or China stone (mixed)	$\left. \begin{array}{l} ·030\ MgO \\ ·180\ CaO \\ ·315\ K_2O \\ ·143\ Na_2O \end{array} \right\} \begin{array}{l} Al_2O_3 ; \\ 7·15\ SiO_2 \end{array}$	582		1300°
Felspar (potash)	$K_2O. Al_2O_3. 6SiO_2$	556		1200°
Felspar (soda)	$N_2O. Al_2O_3. 6SiO_2$	524	See albite.	
Felspar (lime)	$CaO. Al_2O_3. 2SiO_2$	278	See anorthite.	
Flint	SiO	60	Acid substance.	1830°
Fluospar	CaF_2	78		1400°
Ferric oxide (iron)	Fe_2O_3	160	Most universal pigment in glazes. Gives creams, yellows, browns, black, celadons.	
Ferrous oxide (iron)	FeO	72	Gives blue and green tints. Is obtained by reduction of Fe_2O_3 in kilns. Celadons.	
Ferrosic oxide (magnetic)	Fe_3O_4	232		
Fireclay			Refractory clay.	
Iron (see above)				

	Symbol	Molecular Weight	Remarks	Fusing Point
Jersey stone	$\cdot 117$ CaO $\rbrace$ Al$_2$O$_3$ $\cdot 343$ K$_2$O $\rbrace$ 10SiO$_2$ $\cdot 477$ Na$_2$O	770		
Kaolin	Al$_2$O$_3$. 2SiO$_2$. 2H$_2$O	258		
Lead oxide	PbO	223	Basic.	
Lead carbonate	PbCO$_3$	267	Basic.	
Lead carbonate (white lead)	3 PbO. H$_2$O. 2CO$_2$	775	Basic.	
Lead oxide (red lead)	Pb$_3$O$_4$	685	Basic.	
Lead sulphide (galena)	PbS	239	Basic.	
Lynn sand (silica)	SiO$_2$	60	Acid substance.	
Limestone (calcium carbonate)	CaCO$_3$	100		
Limespar	CaO. Al$_2$O$_3$. 2SiO$_2$	278·6		
Magnesia carbonate	MgCO$_3$	84·3		
Manganese dioxide (black)	MnO$_2$	87		
Nickel oxide	NiO	74·7		
Potash (potassium oxide)	K$_2$O	94		
Potassium carbonate	K$_2$CO$_3$	138		
Quartz	SiO$_2$	60		
Rutile	TiO$_2$	80	A crude oxide of titanium.	
Salt	NaCl	58·5		800°
Silica	SiO$_2$	60		
Silver sand (silica)	SiO$_2$	60		
Sodium oxide	Na$_2$O	62		
Sodium carbonate (anhydrous)	Na$_2$CO$_3$	106	Used for casting slips. (*Soda ash*).	
Sodium silicate	Na$_3$Si$_4$O$_4$	122	Used for casting slips.	
Steatite (talc)	3 MgO. 4SiO$_2$. H$_2$O			
Stannic oxide (tin oxide)	SnO$_2$	151	Gives opaque white in colours and glazes.	
Stannous oxide	SnO	135		
Soapstone (talc or steatite)	3MgO. 4SiO$_2$. H$_2$O	378·9		
Strontium oxide	SrO	104		
Tin oxide (see stannic oxide)	SnO$_2$	151		
Titanium dioxide	TiO$_2$	80		
Uranium oxide	UO$_2$	270·5		
Whiting (calcium)	CaCO$_3$	100	Basic.	
Zinc oxide	ZnO	81	Gives opaque white in certain glazes. Brightens colours, especially blue.	

In the chemical formula of a glaze there are three divisions, each of which expresses a distinct function. On the left hand are the bases, which are the fluxes ; these indicate the nature of the glaze, such as lead, lime or alkaline glaze, etc. As all glazes are silicates, or silcates and borates, this is the usual way of distinguishing them. In the middle is the alumina or amphoteric ; these regulate the behaviour of the glaze during firing, making it more viscous or sluggish and preventing a too-rapid flow. At the right hand stand the acids (the chief being silica), the dominating factor with which all the other ingredients combine, and which controls the behaviour of the glaze as a whole, raising or lowering its melting-point, and regulating the fitting of the glaze to the body. In the following table giving the basis in order of fusibility and setting out the various oxides in their three divisions, R stands for the metal.

Basic RO/R_2O	Amphoteric R_2O_3	Acidic RO_2
PbO	Al_2O_3	SiO_2
BaO	Fe_2O_3	B_2O_3
K_2O	Cr_2O_3	TiO_2
Na_2O		SnO_2
ZnO		
CaO		
MgO		

From the foregoing, it will be understood that glazes must have acids and bases, as also have clays. Silica is the potter's chief acid substance, for it combines readily with bases under heat. Boric acid being more fusible than silica is only used in soft glazes, e.g. those having a lower maturing point.

Some important factors about glazes. A glaze being made by combining certain of the bases with the acid substances, the proportion of acid to base is variable within limits. A glaze must be a bi-silicate ; having more than one equivalent of acid to one equivalent of base. The molecular weights represent the proportion in which they combine. One or more bases may be used, but the more bases used produce a more fusible glass. The bases must always total unity. Lead is the only satisfactory base used alone, although it is possible to use soda in this respect.

Much of the skill of glaze-making lies in selecting the various materials to fit the formula. It will readily be seen that it is possible to work out many recipes to fit the same formula ; each recipe giving a somewhat different glaze, some of which would be suitable for one body and some for others. On the other hand many recipes, which may be quite different from one another may be found to be very similar in formula. It will also be seen that a vast field of experiment lies between the limiting formulae of the bases—alumina-silica ratio, but a vaster unlimited and uncontrolled field lies in permuting the figures of the recipe. Thus the usefulness of the formula lies in the adjustment of glazes through it, as

The proportion of alumina is usually one-tenth to one-sixth to that of the acid. In most glazes several bases are used. The behaviour of the glaze is affected by the number of bases used, and also the kind of bases used.

THE ALUMINA—SILICA RATIO

Typical formulae for various kinds of ware

Maturing temperature required	Type of glaze	Type of ware	Formula		
			Bases	Amphoteric	Acids
900° to 1150° centigrade	Raw	Coarse earthenwares. Terracotta	RO.	$0.0 — 0.3\ R_2O_3.$	$1.75 — 3.0\ SiO_2.$
1150° to 1300° centigrade	Raw	Stoneware	RO.	$0.2 — 0.6\ R_2O_3.$	$2.0 — 5.0\ SiO_2.$
1300° to 1500° centigrade	Raw	Hard paste porcelain	RO.	$0.5 — 1.2\ R_2O_3.$	$6.0 — 12.0\ SiO_2.$
1000° to 1200° centigrade	Fritted	Bartheware. Faience. Enamels	RO.	$0.0 — 0.3\ R_2O_3.$	$2.0 — 4.0\ SiO_2.\ 0.5\ SnO_2.$
1000° to 1200° centigrade	Fritted	Fine earthenware. China. Soft paste porcelain	RO.	$0.1 — 0.4\ R_2O_3.$	$2.0 — 4.0\ SiO_2.$ $0.0 — 0.5\ B_2O_3.$

given recipes will need adjustment if they are to fit the different conditions brought about by the use of different bodies, firing conditions and ingredients from different sources. Only practical testing and adjustment will give success.

A simple form of lead glaze having the formula :— PbO $\cdot 2Al_2O_3$ $1\cdot75SiO_2$ could be worked into a recipe as follows, using lead oxide (litharge) china clay, flint.

PbO	Al_2O_3	SiO_2	Raw materials	Molecular Parts	Molecular Weights	Parts by weights or recipe	%
1			Litharge	1	× 223 =	223	62·6
	·2	·4	China clay	·2	× 258 =	52	14·6
		1·35	Flint	1·35	× 60 =	81	22·6
1	·2	1·75					99·8

China clay is used in glazes to supply the alumina. It also gives the glaze the necessary adhesion to the ware. The H_2O burns away, so it does not enter into the ultimate composition, but it must be taken into account in calculating the molecular weight of china clay. Flint is practically pure silica, so also is quartz, which could have been used in place of the flint. If white lead (lead carbonate) had been used, $3PbO. H_2O.$ $2CO_2$ molecular weight 775, the reading would be as follows, as only ·33 molecular parts of white lead are required to give one molecular part of PbO.

PbO	Al_2O_3	SiO_2	Raw materials	Molecular parts	Molecular parts	Recipe	%
·33			White lead	·33	× 775 =	258	63
	·2	·4	China clay	·2	× 258 =	52	14
		1·35	Flint	1·35	× 60 =	81	23
·33	·2	1·75					100

Owing to the Poisonous qualities of lead, it would be much better to use it in a fritted form as lead monosilicate. An excellent type of lead glaze with the recipe

65 white lead, 30 flint, 15 Cornish stone

will be found to give better results as the use of Cornish stone brings into the formula other bases as well as supplying alumina and silica

By dividing the recipe parts by the molecular weights of the corresponding materials, the molecular parts of the formula could be found and then by adding together the figures corresponding to the basic oxides, etc., and dividing the results by the total of the bases, to give unity to the bases, the formula would be found.

Thus the stoneware glaze having the recipe

Flint	7·9
Whiting	13·0
China Clay	6·7
Potash Felspar	72·3

would be worked conversely and tabulated. The molecular formula of the main materials being given as follows : potash felspar, K_2O, Al_2O_3, $6SiO_2$; whiting, $CaCO_3$; china clay, Al_2O_3, $2SiO_2$, $2H_2O$; flint, SiO_2. The molecular weight of flint is 60, consequently 7·9 parts by weight introduce $\frac{7·9}{60} = 0·13$ molecular part of the flint, that is of SiO_2. The molecular weight of whiting is 100, consequently $\frac{13·0}{100} = 0·13$ parts of CaO, since the CO_2 is eliminated in the firing of the glaze. The molecular weight of china clay is 258, consequently $\frac{6·7}{258} = 0·025$ part of china clay, but 0·025 molecular part of china clay introduces 0·025 part of Al_2O_3, 0·025 × 2 part of SiO_2, and the same of H_2O which is eliminated in the fire. The molecular part of SiO_2 must be entered into its tabulated column. In the same way, the molecular weight of felspar is 556, consequently $\frac{72·3}{556} = 0·13$ part of felspar, but 0·13 molecular part of felspar introduces 0·13 part of K_2O, 0·13, of Al_2O_2, and 0·13 × 6 = 0·780 part of SiO_2. Tabulating the results we obtain :—

Material	Molecular weight	Recipe or parts by weight	Molecular parts	K_2O	CaO	Al_2O_3	SiO_2
Flint	60	7·9	·130				·130
Whiting	100	13·0	·130		·130		
China clay	258	6·7	·025			·025	·050
Potash felspar	556	72·3	·130	·130		·130	·780
				·130	·130	·155	·960

The formula thus obtained is therefore

$$\left.\begin{array}{l} ·130 \ K_2O \\ ·130 \ CaO \end{array}\right\} ·155 \ Al_2O_3, \ ·960 \ SiO_2$$

The sum of the bases is ·260. If we divide the coefficient of each oxide by this quantity, we obtain the unity of the bases and the corresponding balance of the glaze : in the following formula

$$\left.\begin{array}{l} ·5 \ K_2O \\ ·5 \ CaO \end{array}\right\} ·6 \ Al_2O_3, \ 3·7 \ SiO_2$$

For greater accuracy the percentage composition from analysis of the materials should be used, where these are available. When unavailable, one can only assume ideal proportions. Rules for this calculation are :—
(a) Find the percentage chemical composition of each material used in the recipe, and set out in tabular form the proportion of each constituent.

)b) Add together the figures of all the same constituents when they occur in different ingredients in the recipe, so as to find the total proportion of each constituent.

(c) Divide the total amount of each constituent by its molecular weight.

(d) Rearrange the results in the order, bases, amphoteric, acid.

(e) Divide the results of (d) by the total of the bases, so as to bring the bases to unity.

This method of calculation is of the greatest value when the accurate composition of the raw materials is known. In trying out different recipes, it may be found that they give almost identical results in the kiln. Formulae can explain that and errors in the composition may often be corrected in a manner impossible otherwise. Despite these advantages, there are many disadvantages in the use of formulae, variations in the composition of the raw materials can be troublesome and, in some cases, minute quantities of ingredients present in the raw materials, which may be too small to be included in the formula, can influence the glaze. Nevertheless, the use of formulae in sorting out recipes into various classes, gives the glazer a basis upon which to work, and a system upon which to build up a glaze, and above all, knowledge of what he is doing ; without this, bewilderment and disappointment can only ensue.

Raw materials for glazes. The materials used should be carefully chosen so as to ensure a glaze maturing at the right temperature, and having the desired properties. This is important with regard to materials supplying the fluxes ; potash, for example, would supply a more fusible glaze if added as a soluble compound than if it were added in the insoluble form of felspar or Cornish stone ; but if it is not desired to frit the materials, only insoluble substances can be used, as the glaze would unmix itself on the surface of the pot. The following are some of the principal materials used in glazes.

Lead oxide may be used in the form of red lead, white lead, litharge, galena, lead monosilicate (a fritted form of lead).

Potash may be introduced in the form of felspar, Cornish stone, potash or nitre or in the form of wood ash.

Soda may be used in the form of soda, borax, soda felspar (albite), common salt.

Zinc oxide in the form of the oxide.

Magnesia in the form of the oxide, magnesite (magnesium carbonate) or talc.

Barium in the form of witherite (barium carbonate) or barytes.

Calcium in the form of whiting (calcium carbonate), or borocalcite.

Alumina may be introduced through many sources, chiefly china clay or other clays, felspar, Cornish stone and other alumina-silicates.

Silica is introduced in the form of free silica through flint, quartz, sand, and in the combined state, through clay, felspar, stone and other silicates and alumina-silicates.

Boric acid may be introduced through boric acid, borax, borocalcite.

Fritted glazes and calculations. Fritted glazes consist of those in which part of the constituent materials are soluble in water, such as borax, soda, etc. These materials are fused or fritted with part of the insoluble materials composing the glaze. This pre-melting of the soluble parts with some of the insoluble parts of the glaze, renders the resultant frit insoluble. The frit is then mixed and ground with the remainder of the insoluble constituent materials, making the final glaze mixture.

It is not good practice to frit all the materials together both soluble and insoluble as a wholly fritted glaze does not suspend well in water, and also it is a costly business : but fritting does ensure a more homogeneous material.

The use of frits—fritting. Various frits may be purchased from potters' suppliers, but it is not usual to disclose the composition of them, therefore users are at a great disadvantage. Frits are usually of two kinds ; alkaline frits and boracic frits. These two kinds produce different colours when stained, so that when a glaze of a particular tint is required, a frit of the suitable composition should be used. Frits are usually prepared in a special furnace of the reverberating type. When the molten mass is fluid, it is run off into cold water and afterwards ground in a porcelain ball mill. When only a small quantity of frit is required, a crucible may be used ; or a saggar may be used and heated along with other saggars containing ware. When a crucible or saggar is used, it should have its inner surface rubbed with finely ground flint, so as to prevent adhesion of the frit. The saggars must be broken and separated from the frit, and care taken to remove all particles of saggar or crucible material from the frit. The time of fritting should be as short as possible as they lose alkali and become less fusible by prolonged heating ; nor should the temperature be higher than is necessary.

TYPICAL FRITS

Alkaline frits	1	2	Boracic frits	1	2	3
Flint	64	66	Cornish stone	4		16
Nitre	14		Flint	8	16	16
Soda	7	20	Borax	20	20	30
Whiting	15	14	Whiting	4	8	16
			China clay		8	16
			Soda	1	4	6

There can be many variations in frit composition, but all should possess the required qualities of insolubility and low melting point. It is usually necessary to include two bases as well as silica, in a frit, to secure insolubility in the glaze. Potash and flint alone do not ensure insolubility unless lime, lead or other suitable base is also present. Fritted glazes are better than raw glazes for certain types of ware ; they are often more shiny and less easily scratched and, as a rule, more fusible and better for use with underglaze colours. As some fritted materials lose a considerable amount of weight by being fritted in the form of water, etc., calculations must be made before the final mixture of frit with the other parts of the glaze can be made. In cases where the loss is unknown, a calculation based on the approximate losses of each constituent may be used. Felspar and flint undergo no loss, but china clay loses its 36 parts of water ; whiting its 44 parts ; and borax loses 180 parts of each equivalent measured by its molecular weight. Put into percentage the following table is of use, where the composition of the materials is invariable.

Material	Loss in weight during fritting
Borax	47·1 per cent
Boric acid	43·5 ,, ,,
Barium carbonate	22·3 ,, ,,
Borocalcite	18·0 ,, ,,
Whiting	44·0 ,, ,,
China clay	14·0 ,, ,,
White lead	13·7 ,, ,,
Magnesium carbonate	52·1 ,, ,,
Nitre	53·5 ,, ,,
Soda ash	41·5 ,, ,,
Soda crystals	78·3 ,, ,,

The following formula

$$·25\ Na_2O \qquad 2·10\ SiO_2$$
$$·20\ K_2O\ \ ·3\ Al_2O_3 \qquad ·50\ B_2O_3$$
$$·30\ CaO$$
$$·25\ PbO$$

could be worked as follows—fritting all the soluble substances with part of the insoluble substances.

	Na_2O	K_2O	CaO	PbO	Al_2O_3	SiO_2	B_2O_3
Original formula of glaze ...	·25	·20	·30	·25	·30	2·10	·50
Formula of frit	·25	·10	·30		·20	1·10	·50
Formula to be added to the frit at the mill mixture ...		·10		·25	·10	1·0	

Table for the calculation of the frit mixture

Na_2O	K_2O	CaO	Al_2O_3	SiO_2	B_2O_3	Raw materials	Mol. pts.	Mol. wts.	Parts by weight
·25					·50	Borax	·25	382 =	95·5
	·10		·10	·60		Potash felspar	·10	556 =	55·6
		·30				Whiting	·30	100 =	30·0
			·10	·20		China clay	·10	258 =	25·8
				·30		Flint	·30	60 =	18·0
·25	·10	·30	·20	1·10	·50				224·9

The frit mixture is therefore
    95·5 Borax
    55·6 Potash felspar
    30·0 Whiting
    25·8 China clay
    18·0 Flint
    ——
    224·9

Table for the calculation of the remainder of the glaze formula

K_2O	PbO	Al_2O_3	SiO_2	Raw materials	Mol. pts.	Mol. wts.	Parts by weight
·10		·10	·60	Potash felspar	·10	556 =	55·6
	·25			Lead carbonate	·25	267 =	66·75
			·40	Flint	·40	60 =	24·0
·10	·25	·10	1·0				146·35

According to the conversion table of loss in weight during fritting :—

99·5 parts of Borax brings in after fritting $\dfrac{95 \cdot 5 \ (100 - 47 \cdot 1)}{100}$ = 50·500

55·6 ,, ,, Felspar ,, ,, ,,   = 55·600
30·0 ,, ,, Whiting ,, ,, ,, $\dfrac{30 \cdot 0 \ (100 - 44)}{100}$ = 16·800

25·8 ,, ,, China clay ,, ,, $\dfrac{25 \cdot 8 \ (100 - 14)}{100}$ = 22·188

18·0 ,, ,, Flint ,, ,, ,,   = 18·00
                                     ——————
                                     163·088

Since 224·9 parts of frit mixture are found to give 163·088 parts of frit, the recipe of the mill mixture is :—
    163·088 Frit
    55·600 Potash felspar
    66·750 Lead carbonate
    24·000 Flint

Matt glazes may be obtained by a number of means, and are known by the definitions which indicate the type : alumina matt, zinc matt, lime matt, etc.

In soft matt glazes, the silica should be kept low, boracic acid absent, and the alumina as high as possible. Zinc oxide does most of the work in matting a glaze.

Applied to a soft glaze, these principles would give :—

$$0.15 \text{ CaO}$$
$$0.35 \text{ ZnO} \quad 0.28 \text{ Al}_2\text{O}_3 \quad 1.5 \text{ SiO}_2.$$
$$0.50 \text{ PbO}$$

CaO	ZnO	PbO	Al$_2$O$_3$	SiO$_2$	Raw materials	Mol. pts.	Mol. wts.	Recipe	
·15					Whiting	·15	100	15·00	
	·35				Zinc oxide	·35	81	28·35	Raw glaze
		·50			Lead oxide	·50	223	111·50	
			·28	·56	China clay	·28	258	72·24	
				·94	Flint	·94	60	56·40	
·15	·35	·50	·28	1·50					

Lime matts can be simply produced by adding about twenty per cent of whiting to almost any glaze. Barium matt by putting in about 0·25 BaO into the bases and the alumina ratio high. The firing range is narrow in this case, but certain colour effects can be obtained. Matt glazes require applying to the pottery rather thickly to obtain the best results, but the insides of pieces of ware to be used for food are best coated with a shiny glaze, as matt glazes are not so hygienic as shiny ones.

Stoneware glazes. Stoneware may be glazed in several different ways. The body may be fired to produce a hard biscuit and then glazed with any of the glazes used for earthenware. It is often glazed in the green or unfired state, after which, body and glaze are matured at the same heat. In practice it is much better to fire the body sufficiently hard enough (about 950°C) to enable it to be handled with ease. The same practice applies to hard porcelain as, in both cases, glaze and body mature together. The type known as Bristol glazes which consist chiefly of zinc, lime and potash bases give excellent results.

Stoneware glazes recipes. Temperatures 1250° to 1300°

		Semi-opaque		Matt	Bristol tpye					
Felspar (potash)	40·22		72·0	41·75	55·6	67·0	58·0	40·0	75·0	
Whiting	9·64	10·91	13·0	17·50	10·0	7·0	8·0	20·0	15·0	20·0
Barium carbonate	14·25									
China clay	14·10	5·67	7·0	25·75	8·6	9·0	14·0	10·0		9·0
Flint	21·70	6·55	8·0		18·0	4·0	8·0	30·0		6·0
Cornish stone									10·0	65·0
Zinc oxide		70·35			10·8	11·0	10·0			
Tin oxide		4·50								

All the above glazes are leadless, as lead cannot be used above 1150°C, and they are all raw glazes.

Salt glaze. On a suitable stoneware body, which must be vitreous and highly siliceous, a glaze may be produced by throwing salt into the kiln towards the end of firing. This method was in use in the Rhineland in the twelfth century, but its use nowadays is mainly confined to drain pipes. In salt glazing, the common salt is decomposed by the heat (usually about 1250°) forming sodium oxide (Na_2O) and hydrochloric acid (HCl). The sodium oxide combines with the silica and alumina in the clay of the ware, forming a glaze; the acid escapes in the form of vapour. It can usually be identified by a slight orange-peel texture, although this was often eliminated by coating the ware before firing with an engobe of white burning clay and flint.

Porcelain glazes. For the softer type of porcelain firing, at between 1280° and 1320°, I have found the following formula to give excellent results :—

$$
\begin{array}{ll}
CaO & \cdot 61 \\
K_2O & \cdot 15 \quad 0\cdot 55\ Al_2O_3 ;\quad 4\cdot 5\ SiO_2 \\
Na_2O & \cdot 15 \\
BaO & \cdot 09
\end{array}
$$

Recipe.

Limestone	12·200—
Potash felspar	16·680—
Soda felspar	16·180—
Barium carbonate	3·546—raw materials.
China clay	12·900—
Quartz	26·600—

A very simple recipe can be found in a balance of Cornish stone and whiting in varying proportions.

Cornish stone | 8 | 10 |

Whiting | 1 | 2 | The stone supplying the various bases, alumina and silica—the whiting providing the additional flux. These glazes can also be applied with good results on stoneware bodies. A reduction in maturing temperature could be effected by using borocalcite.

Opaque and coloured glazes. Glazes are usually rendered opaque by the addition of tin oxide in varying percentages from about four to ten per cent but other opacifying agents are used. A glaze may be opaque owing to undissolved particles in the glaze which might become clear at a higher temperature. If a frit is used the opacifying agent should be introduced into the mill mixture and not fritted. In the realm of coloured glazes is a wide field giving scope for individual expression. All glazes can be coloured, but it must be remembered that different glazes produce different colours from the same colouring oxide. Not only do the various bases influence the particular colouring metal, but also do the percentage of colour used and the atmosphere in the kiln, whether reducing or oxidising.

Also the presence of boric acid ; tin will affect certain colours. Thus copper in a lead glaze will give grass greens ; in an alkaline glaze the lovely Egyptian and Persian blues, whilst in a porcelain glaze and in a reducing atmosphere, it will give the copper reds of the Chinese. Similarly iron oxide in small percentages will give creamy and honey-coloured glazes when oxidised. If reduced in leadless glazes, fine celadons are obtained. It will readily be understood that the whole matter is one of testing through the medium of the fire, although certain guides can be given.

Colour modifications due to variations in glaze compositions.

Colourant	% of Colour to transparent glazes	Lead glazes	Alkaline glazes	
Oxide of copper	0·5 to 5·0	Grass greens	Turquoise	Red in a reducing fire.
Oxide of cobalt	0·5 to 4·0	Blue	Blue	Pink in magnesia glazes.
Oxide of chrome	0·1 to 0·4	Yellow green	Green	Opaque greens. A higher percentage in leadless glaze.
Oxide of iron	1·0 to 10·0	Yellow brown	Brown to blackish	Celadon greens in a reducing fire 1 to 3 per cent in leadless glazes — Aventurine effects in rich boracic glazes.
Oxide of manganese	1·0 to 4·0	Claret brown	Violet	Use $BaCO_3$ if violets are required.
Oxide of nickel	0·1 to 0·5	Straw brown	Brown	Unpleasant colour.
Oxide of uranium	1·0 to 6·0	Yellow	Orange yellow	
Oxide of tin	4·0 to 10·0	White	White	

The oxides may be mixed to give various tints. Rutile will give broken matt effect. When introducing colour into a transparent colourless glaze, it should be remembered that the addition of colour usually affects the melting point and coefficient of the glaze, so that the composition of the glaze may have to be adjusted accordingly. The addition of a colouring oxide usually makes the glaze more fusible but, if only a small amount of colour is needed, this could be ignored. Tests however should always be made.

Glaze faults. While it may happen that body and glaze and firing are so mutually adjusted that faults are absent, this is the exception instead of the rule, unless by careful adjustment the faults have been eliminated. The expansion on heating and shrinkage on cooling of ceramic materials, which may not neutralise each other, may cause crazing, peeling or other defects.

Crazing. This is a sign that the glaze does not fit the body and means that the composition of the glaze must be altered so that its coefficient of expansion corresponds more closely to that of the body. A little flint added to the body or glaze may ease the trouble, but it must be remembered that the addition of flint to the glaze will render it less fusible. The substitution of a base of high molecular weight for one of a lower molecular weight will increase the coefficient of expansion. Sometimes underfiring of the body or overfiring of the glaze induces crazes. Crazing does not always take place immediately upon cooling, but may happen days or weeks after firing.

Peeling. Indicates the reverse of crazing. Its symptoms are the glazed edges of the ware flaking off. The remedy is the reverse of that of crazing.

Crawling or Ruckling—leaving bald patches. This may be caused by overgrinding of the glaze, underfiring of the body, too much clay in the glaze or overglazing (too thick a layer of glaze).

Blistering. This is usually caused by bubbles of gas produced during firing. They may be eliminated by a highly oxidising atmosphere. They may be caused by sulphur compounds in the body being unable to escape through the viscous glaze. Often, refiring will eliminate blistering. Care should be taken to ensure clean biscuit ware free from grease, dust or damp spots. It is good practice to brush the ware before glazing.

VIII. Enamel or on-glaze decoration

At this final stage in the production of a piece of pottery, the same metallic colours can be applied in various ways. They are, however, mixed with a flux, usually of red lead, borax and flint, in order to fix them to the glazed surface of the pottery and to give them glossiness. The range of colours is the most extensive of all ceramic palettes ; fine reds, pinks and delicate pastel tints are available for, owing to the comparatively low temperature at which they are fired on to the ware (from 700° to 950° centigrade), many more metals can be used than is possible for underglaze. Yet they never have the same quality as the underglaze colours.

The extensive range of colours and their reliability, together with the ease with which they can be applied and the fact that they can be cleaned off the ware before firing in case of error, make them a convenient commercial method of decoration, and so we find that the bulk of commercial pottery is decorated by the on-glaze methods. For direct painting they are applied by the turpentine and fat oil medium as in underglaze painting.

Sometimes oil of lavender or aniseed is used to further the manipulation of the colours. These latter may be sprayed upon the surface of the ware or printed from copper plates (see Printing) and they are used extensively in on-glaze lithography. Camel hair brushes as supplied by the potters' colourmen are the best for painting in enamels, as the oily medium stiffens them and they are capable of holding a good body of colour. They are obtainable in various shapes and sizes, liners, tracers, shaders, etc. Lines and bands are executed on the lining wheel exactly as in underglaze painting.

Groundlaying. Flat grounds of enamel colour can be laid by first coating the ware with a special groundlaying oil thinned down with turpentine. Only a thin coating is needed and this should be applied with a flat brush. When it has become tacky, it should be dabbled lightly with a silk boss (a small pad of cotton wool covered with Jap silk) ; this ensures an even coating. Then, with a clean piece of cotton wool, the colour is dusted on lavishly. The colour will adhere to the sticky surface, and after it has dried for a while, the edges may be cleaned up, and pattern can be swiftly drawn through the colour, giving the effect of a white line-drawing similar to a scraper-board technique ; or the ground can be left flat and fired, after which it may be painted on again (see plates XXXVI and XXXVII). Any parts to which the colour must not adhere, may previously be covered with a water colour mixed with sugar or treacle. After the colour has been dusted on, the article may be plunged into cold water which dissolves and washes away the protecting matter, but leaves the parts coated with oil and colour, unharmed.

Gold, silver, pink and oxidised lustres. On the fired glaze and at enamel kiln temperatures, metallic effects may be produced by applying gold, silver and other precious metal preparations. They can be bought ready for use and are easy to apply by brushwork. They can be used in combination with colour work, but an important point in the firing of these in the enamel kiln is that the doors of the kiln should be left open until the kiln is well heated in order to allow the fumes to escape, otherwise the lustres will be sulphured. If the wares are coated all over with the metals, they will, of course, have a metallic effect which will be wrong æsthetically. A more correct use of silver is known as the *resist process,* which gives a white pattern on a silvered ground (*see plate XXXIX*). To effect this, the ware should be cleaned with a little whiting powder and the pattern painted in glycerine or similar substance. Ordinary vermilion water-colour works quite well, and the pattern can easily be seen, but it must be painted on thickly. This acts as a resist, so that the whole piece can then be covered by the silver solution, which should not be applied too thickly. Before firing, it is of a nut brown colour. After drying and before firing, the piece may be washed with water, which detaches the glycerine preparation leaving the white pattern, or it may be fired first, and then polished with whiting, which removes the resist and reveals the white pattern on the silvered ground. Thin lines may be scratched out with a steel point before firing. Other lustres may be treated in this manner. One has only to visit our museums in order to see to what excellent use the Staffordshire potters put this process.

Reduced lustres. Anyone familiar with the lovely iridescent colourings of the Persian, Hispano-Moresque and Italian pots, cannot fail to be charmed by the results of this process. The reducing atmosphere of the firing causes an extremely thin film of metal to be deposited on the surface of the ware, thus producing the iridescence. The pottery is first produced into the fired glaze state and an alkaline glaze, or one having a small percentage of lead rendered opaque by the addition of tin oxide, should be used. Upon this the painting is executed. The colouring agents, copper oxide, silver oxide, are mixed with a vehicle of dried china clay or red clay, to which may be added a little treacle or gum arabic to cause adhesion to the ware, and help in reduction. This pigment is then used for the painting. Much of the pigment coating will be removed after the firing by rubbing, leaving the thin film of metal. The smoking or reducing of the pigment must be produced at the exact moment when the metals commence to volatilise ; at about 600° centigrade, just when the kiln is beginning to show colour. This third firing should be oxidising up to this point, and reduction kept up for about fifteen minutes. Reduction may be effected by means of resinous wood thrown into the muffle, or by introducing coal gas. The smoke-covered ware, after cooling, must be washed and rubbed before the lustre can be seen.

Red clay ...	...	...	...	...	100		
China clay	...	...	...	...		100	100
Carbonate of copper	...	...	...	25	30	
Carbonate of silver	...	...	...	$1\frac{1}{4}$	2	
Sulphide of copper	...	...	...			50

On-glaze printing from copper plates. This is very similar to under-glaze or biscuit printing, except that the engraved line need not be so deep and that a slightly different mixture of oil is used and also the glazed surface of the ware needs a varnish to ensure the transfer print sticking to it. All the materials involved can be obtained from potters' suppliers. After printing on to the glost surface, the pottery requires firing to enamel temperature (about 800° centigrade) to fix the colour, as enamel colours and not underglaze colours are used in this case.

In the pottery industry where large quantities of prints are required, a press is used as mentioned in Chapter VI, having an engraved roller. This produces a continuous pattern, printed on lengths of paper, in a similar manner to the method used for machine printed textiles.

Other methods of decorating pottery. *Tin enamel.* Apart from the three principal stages at which pottery can be decorated, slips on the clay state, underglaze on the biscuit, and enamels on the fired glaze, decoration can also be applied on the unfired glaze. This was the technique employed by the Italian and Dutch pottery painters. For painting on tin glaze special stanniferous colours may be purchased and used, but excellent results can be obtained by using the raw oxides : cobalt giving intense blues; iron, reddish brown; manganese, purples; copper, greens, and antimoniate of lead, yellows. These may be mixed with a little tin glaze to give them body and glossiness, or the whole of the painting and background can be sprayed with a little clear glaze before firing. The technique of painting on the unfired glaze is a little difficult, as the glaze is rather powdery when dry, and is apt to pick up on to the brush, but this may be overcome by coating the glaze with a thin film of gum tragacanth, which gives a firm surface. The gum, like all other siccatives and suspenders, burns away. For the best effects, the painting should be executed with swift, dexterous strokes, and if possible, avoid retouching. The Italian Majolica painters used the system of first painting the whole of the design in cobalt, and over this foundation were laid the other colours, yellow, green, purple, etc. There is much to be said for this method, as blue is the most dependable of all ceramic colours and is greatly assisted by the tin glaze, so that if the other colours might burn away a little, the blue could always be depended on to give a complete rendering, assisted by what remained of the other colours.

Tin glaze recipes to fire at about 980° centigrade.

Lead monosilicate	80	68		
Cornish stone	15			
China clay		4		or any other clear glaze
Felspar (potash)		10		+ 6% to 10% tin oxide.
Whiting			5	
Flint	5	10	20	
Oxide of tin	8	8	10	
Wengers ⎰ 714 Frit			50	
⎱ 902 ,,			10	

Stonewares and porcelain. The same technique of painting on the unfired glaze may be followed with excellent results on stoneware glazes, the pigments in this case being confined to iron, copper and cobalt. At stoneware heats, the metallic oxides require no glaze mixing with them, as the high fire causes them to sink into the glaze, and melts them sufficiently to become glossy. Iron alone gives fine rust reds to brownish blacks, according to the strength at which it is applied. A minute percentage of cobalt mixed with the iron pigment produces a fine blackish colour. Copper, if reduced, will give fine copper reds. A little china clay added to the pigments greatly assists their stability. The student would do well to study the fine wares of the Sung dynasty, particularly the Tzechow wares.

Another interesting form of decoration is cut glaze. For this purpose, only glazes which are still, and do not run, can be used. I have used stoneware glazes applied on to the unfired clay with great effect in this manner, particularly the stoneware black glaze of 88 Cornish stone, 12 whiting, 8 red oxide of iron, fired at 1280° centigrade with a reducing atmosphere. This ware is only once fired, body and glaze maturing together. To assist glazing the raw clay, which is first dried, some gelatine is added to the glaze, which may then be brushed on in several coats, building up a good thickness of glaze. The glaze can then be cut through to the body of the pot after the manner of the Tzechow cut glaze stonewares.

Other treatments. In some treatments of raised line slip work, the interspaces are filled in with different coloured glazes, the raised line acting as a dam to keep the different colours separate, otherwise the glazes would run into each other during the glaze firing. The whole effect is similar to cloisonné enamels, and is capable of beautiful treatment. Some of the wares of the Ming dynasty were decorated in this manner. A further use of slip which originated in China, is the *paté-sur-paté* method. In this case, fairly high relief designs are obtained by building up the slip by brushing, supplemented by the use of modelling tools. It is thus a combination of both painting and modelling. For the best effects, translucent bodies must be used, covered with transparent glazes.

IX. Ceramic lithography

This process is used extensively in the industry, and has partly replaced painting on pottery (*see plate XXXVIII*). Its immense possibilities have not always been artistically used to the best advantage, for much of the work has been purely imitative of painting. It is essentially a mass-production method, and like all other such methods, it rests upon those responsible for the conception and control of the design as to what is produced.

Against the mass-production of beauty there can be no argument; it is only the production of ugliness which is wrong. It will be found, by experience, that it is just as easy and as cheap to produce good designs as bad ones. In this process, as in any other medium, there are limitations necessarily enforced by the process, but there are distinct advantages also. It can be used for monochrome or polychrome decoration, but of course the medium can be best exploited in several colours.

The process follows the same course as in ordinary lithography up to a certain point, when a transfer is made. The design is drawn upon a smooth lithographic stone, with black lithographic chalk or ink, bearing in mind that the design on the stone appears, on account of its transfer, exactly as it will appear on the pottery, and not reversed, as would be the case of printing on paper. The stone is then etched with diluted nitric acid in the usual way. For those not familiar with the process, the method is as follows :—

To prepare the stone. Dust the stone on which the drawing is to be made, with powdered glass and sprinkle this with water until well mottled ; grind with a smaller stone or levigator to give a fine texture. The stone must be quite flat.

Fixing or etching the stone. After the drawing has been made, the whole surface of the stone is dabbed over with a sponge containing 50 parts gum (arabic) and one part nitric acid. Let it rest in this for twelve hours. The gum and acid will sink into every unworked part of the stone which partly becomes nitrified. Nitrified limestone is not sensitive to grease.

Proving the stone. Wash off the gum with sponge and water. Roll up on top of the existing drawing with printing ink. Never let the stone become dry ; it must be kept slightly moist. When the drawing on the stone looks dark enough, take a print : if not dark enough, continue rolling until it gives a good print. Then dry the stone with a fan, and dust it with powdered resin on cotton wool and also dust it with French chalk. Wipe off superfluous resin and chalk with cotton wool. With strong nitric acid, five parts, to one part water, ' boil ' the edges of the stone, but do not let this strong acid touch the work ; squeeze water all over and mop up the strong acid on the edges of the stone with a sponge —squeeze this over the drawing. Keep squeezing weak acid all over the stone several times, and then wash off with clean water. Dry the stone with rag and fan. Rub in pure gum (arabic) with the palm of the hand until this becomes dry, leaving this on for an hour or more. Wash off gum with water and then wash out the work with turpentine. Roll up as before and when the work has come up to full strength it is ready to begin printing in ceramic colours. If the ceramic transfers are to be in several colours, as many prints as there are colours must be taken from the inked stone. These impressions are transferred to other stones, by putting them through the press, and on each stone that part which is to be printed in one colour, is drawn or painted with lithographic ink, and the remainder of the drawing obliterated. Each stone will then have to be etched in the same way as the original stone. To ensure the prints from the different colours registering properly, small crosses may be drawn on the corners of the original stone, so that when the print is laid on each stone for its particular colour, it will register accurately in its correct place.

To print in ceramic colour, special ceramic lithographic paper is needed. The quality known as Duplex Lithographic transfer paper should be used. This is a film of specially prepared tissue paper, backed with a stiffer paper. At this stage, the first stone for printing is washed with turpentine : this removes the inked drawing. It is then sponged with water and rolled up with a glazed roller charged with special ceramic lithographic varnish. If this is too thick and tacky, it may be thinned down with a drop or two of boiled linseed oil. Only an extremely thin film of varnish is required. Fan the stone dry and putting the Duplex paper face down on the stone, put it through the press. A print in varnish will be the result. On this, dust the ceramic colour with cotton wool, the colour will adhere to the varnish. Allow this to dry for twenty-four hours after which the print may be cleaned by wiping with cotton wool and a little fine sawdust. It is then ready for the second stone, from which it is again printed in varnish, and dusted with the second colour as before, allowing to dry and again cleaning before any other colours are printed ; and so on until the whole design has been printed upon the sheet. In order to obtain dark shades of colour, it is necessary to print the same colour several times over the same sheet. If the transfers are to be kept for any time they may be coated with varnish by rolling up a clean stone with varnish, placing the transfers face down on the stone and putting through the press with a light pressure. After drying they can be stacked together and kept for some time, the varnish preventing rubbing.

Transferring the print to the ware. To put the transfers on to the pottery : the ware, in the case of enamel colours, is first coated with a thin film of ceramic litho size, thinned with turpentine if necessary. This is allowed to become tacky. The transfer is stripped of its stiff paper backing, placed in position face down, and rubbed on with a piece of cloth, sponge or roller. It can be further rubbed with a sponge lubricated with a little soap, this ensures perfect contact. It is then damped with water, which penetrates the tissue paper, and acting on its gum coating, renders it soluble. This causes the paper to peel off, leaving the design on the pottery which after being wiped of any scum around the pattern, is fired at enamel heat.

The advantages of lithographic transfers, to the industry, are that any number of prints of an edition can be produced, and that many colours can be applied to the ware at one operation, always giving uniformity. Zinc plates may be used in place of the stones, and under-glaze as well as on-glaze transfers can be made, but the process lends itself more to the on-glaze method, owing to the rather thin nature of the colourings.

X. Packing and firing

The biscuit fire. Much will depend on the nature of the body used, its temperature required, and the type of kiln used, as to its method of packing and the duration of the firing. In every case the ' green wares ' must be as dry as possible, and the early stages of the firing taken very slowly if undue loss is to be avoided. Wet goods or rapid firing are likely to cause explosions among the pots. It is estimated that there is water in a chemically combined state in clays heated up to 600° or 700° centigrade, and this has to be driven off carefully in the form of steam. If the kiln be an open flame, *saggars* must be used to protect the pots from the fierce heat, but if a muffle is used or an electric furnace, the clay ware can be stacked on fireclay shelves, supported by strong fireclay props (*Fig.* 71). Earthenwares may be embedded in a refined silica sand to counteract warping, but china goods require bedding in powdered flint or alumina. As stonewares and hard paste porcelains are only soft baked (about 900° centigrade) at this stage, they require little assistance in this respect, and can be baked in a open flame or enclosed.

Pottery in the biscuit fire does not stick together and shapes can be placed one on top of the other, or small shapes can be packed within larger ones. Biscuit firing is best proceeded with slowly, up to the required temperature, and the temperature held at its maximum for a short period in order to soak the wares thoroughly.

Temperatures can be judged by using cones, bars or trial rings, or by pyrometers, but these latter instruments are expensive and for schools, or the individual craftsman, cones or bars will suffice. These bend at given temperatures and they can be obtained from the manufacturers to suit all temperatures, with about 20° centigrade difference between the various numbers. It is advisable to place in the kiln several cones with numbers approaching the required temperature, and one above it, in

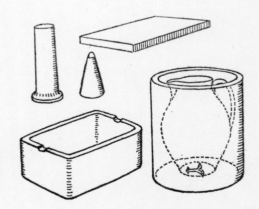

Fig. 71. Kiln furniture: props, shelves and saggars.

order that the rising temperature can be watched, and not exceeded. Cones give approximate temperatures, and are judged to record the particular temperature when half bent (*Fig.* 72).

An excellent spy-hole may be constructed into the brickwork of the kiln door by building in a length of three inch iron piping, partly sawn, with a slot to take a four inch by four inch sheet of mica. This enables one to watch the firing and the cones without having to withdraw a plug (*Fig.* 73).

Fig. 72. *Cones, before and after firing.*

Fig. 73. *A spy-hole of mica slotted into a short length of* 3 *in. pipe.*

The glaze fire. Great care is needed in the packing of wares for this firing, for the pots must not touch each other as the glaze would cause them to stick together. As earthenwares require as complete a glazing as is possible, they must further be balanced on pin points of refractory material in the form of stilts, spurs, etc., (*Figs.* 74 *and* 75). These are procurable in various sizes and shapes to suit all purposes, but skill and ingenuity are needed to pack a kiln economically and with as few stilts or spurs as possible. If an open flame kiln or oven be used, sealed saggars are necessary (*see plates XXXIV and XXXV*), but in a muffle, shelves and props can be used. A little space should be left between the wares, because some glazes are apt to bubble and blister during the fusion of the glaze particles.

Volatile colouring matter in glazes may affect surrounding work, and for this reason should be kept separate. A rapid fire may be used for glazed work, and once the maximum temperature has been reached, it may be immediately relinquished. It is bad practice to attempt to fire biscuit along with glazed wares, as the steam and gases are injurious to the glaze.

The enamel fire. Enamels are nearly always fired in a muffle kiln, but they can be fired in sealed saggars. In this case also, the wares must not touch and they must be balanced on stilts, as the fire, although low in temperature, slightly softens the glaze, and would cause injury to the pieces if they touched. Cracks or crevices in the muffle should be sealed with fireclay stopping, for the fumes have a deleterious affect on the wares. Fireclay shelves and props are used, or cast iron perforated slabs and props of suitable thickness and strength. Enamel kiln heats are usually between 700° and 900° centigrade.

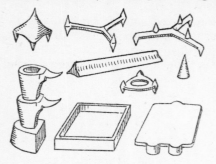

Fig. 74. *Stilts, spurs, saddles and tile boxes for placing wares during the glaze and enamel firings.*

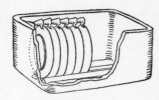

Fig. 75. *The manner of placing plates in saggars for the glaze firing.*

Atmosphere in kilns. The nature of the gaseous atmosphere in kilns has an important influence on the wares being fired, for various effects are produced on the colours and glazes, which may be either oxidised or reduced. In an oxidising atmosphere there is an excess of oxygen present ; in a reducing atmosphere there is a shortage of oxygen; in a neutral atmosphere neither oxidation or reduction can proceed. The phenomena of combustion is either complete or incomplete ; in the former case sufficient, or an excess of oxygen is supplied to oxidise all the fuel. In a reducing fire there is incomplete combustion, and the atmosphere being hungry for oxygen, will abstract it from any source or substance which may present. This affects the colouring oxides present, reducing them to a lower state of oxidation.

Most ceramic articles require an oxidising fire, but certain colouring effects, such as the copper red glazes of the Chinese, and the celadon glazes (produced from reduced iron oxides), as well as all true lustres, require a reducing fire. The colour obtained from copper oxides in an oxidising atmosphere is green or blue-green, according to the nature of the bases used in the glaze, but the same glazes, particularly the high temperature stoneware and porcelain glazes, when reduced, will give copper reds, from a liver colour to an intense blood red. The *sang de bœuf, rouge flambé* and *peach bloom* of the Chinese are excellent examples. In a like manner, about two per cent of iron oxide in a high temperature glaze when oxidised will give warm creams, but if reduced, the cool sea green glazes of great beauty, known as celadons, will result.

The manner of producing a reducing atmosphere varies according to the type of kiln used, but in short, a smoky atmosphere, instead of a clean one, must be produced. In an open flame gas furnace, this is easily achieved by cutting down the air supply to a minimum, and increasing the gas ratio. In the case of a muffle furnace, it may be necessary to introduce into the muffle at the right time resinous wood, in order to create the necessary smoke. The duration of the reducing fire varies accordingly, but it is necessary to reduce the metallic oxides as they begin to volatilise and before the glaze particles fuse ; for, if an impervious skin forms, little reduction can occur. In most materials the most effective reduction occurs between the temperatures 900° and 1000° centigrade.

Approximate temperatures used for different bodies, glazes, etc.

Colour in the kiln.	Heat at which the cone bends in degrees centigrade	Seger cones	
Redness just shows	600	022	
Dull red	650 670 690 710	021 020 019 018	
Red to cherry	730 750 790 815 835 855 880 900	017 016 015A 014A 013A 012A 011A 010A	Enamels. Liquid gold. Silver. Lustres. Hard enamels.
	920	09A	Biscuit for hardpaste porcelain and stoneware.
Dark cherry to Light cherry	940 960 980 1000 1020 1040 1060	08A 07A 06A 05A 04A 03A 02A	Very soft glazes, lead glazes. Tin enamel. Earthenware glaze. Soft china glaze.
Dark orange to Light orange	1080 1100 1120 1140 1160 1180	01A 1A 2A 3A 4A 5A	Earthenware biscuit.
Orange to white	1200 1230 1250 1280	6A 7 8 9	Vitreous ware. Stoneware. Salt glaze.
White	1300 1320 1350	10 11 12	Stoneware glazes. Bone china biscuit. Porcelain glazes. German and Chinese porcelains. Sevres porcelain.
Intense white	1380 1400 1435	13 14 15	
Bluish white	1460 1480 1500	16 17 18	Copenhagen porcelain.

XI. Kilns : types and construction

Without the means of baking, pottery cannot be made, so the kiln or oven forms the most important article of equipment whether the potter be an artist-craftsman, student, or an industrial manufacturer. The heats necessary for the firing of even soft types of pottery are intense. It is therefore important that the best possible type of kiln should always be obtained, for upon it, and its possible heat range, will depend the type of ware to be made. The important factor is the conservation of heat.

There are many types of furnace from the primitive *clamp* kiln, to the modern industrial continuous tunnel oven. All kinds of fuel can be used —wood, coal, coke, oil, gas and electricity. Much depends on the type of fuel available as to what type of kiln should be selected. It is around the kiln that the whole production of the potter revolves, and upon its products he must stand or fall.

Much good work is being done in the construction of electrical furnaces for the baking of pottery, and some excellent small kilns, suitable for schools and experimental work, can be purchased. Electrical kilns are extremely easy to operate and require little attention. They also provide an extremely sweet and clean atmosphere, free from fumes, etc. The chief difficulty in the baking of pottery by electricity lies in the fact that the heating elements do not stand up to high temperatures, although much progress is being made to provide better elements.

In the cases of the other fuels, kilns may be classified as:—kilns for direct firing, and kilns with indirect firing or muffles. Of the former there are :—

(1) **Kilns with horizontal draught,** such as the Newcastle or Cassel kilns. These kilns have a long chamber with a fireplace at one end and a chimney at the other. The flames and hot gases travel amongst the

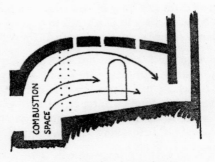

Fig. 76. Horizontal-draught kiln.

wares in the chamber and then pass up the chimney. These kilns are somewhat wasteful in fuel and irregular in heating (*Fig.* 76).

(2) **Round up-draught or rectangular up-draught.** The round up-draught is a common type, generally in use for firing both biscuit and glaze. It consists of a beehive shaped chamber, into which the fire enters at the bottom, rises upwards among the wares, and finally passes away through one or more openings in the roof. The number of fires arranged around the base varies according to the size of the oven. This type sometimes has two chambers, one above the other. These are used for burning porcelain; the bottom chamber for the glaze which requires the most heat, and the upper one for the biscuit which only requires a low remperature. These open flame ovens require saggars to protect the wares from the flames (*Fig.* 77).

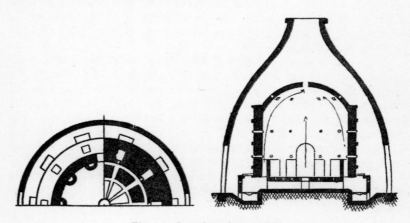

Fig. 77. Round up-draught kiln.

(3) **Rectangular or round down-draught kilns.** In these types the flames are deflected by the dome shaped roof, and are led downwards to pass out through flues in the floor of the kiln, to a main flue connected to the chimney. A down-draught kiln tends to heat up the contents more uniformly, and can be more economical in fuel (*Fig.* 78).

Muffles. In this case the flames do not directly enter the chamber but are led around it by flues, and escape into the chimney. Muffle furnaces are used chiefly for enamelled wares, as it is not possible to attain the high temperatures with a muffled furnace, as it is with an open flame. All these are known as *intermittent* types, as they have to be packed when cold, fired, and cooled off, before they can be emptied.

Continuous kilns. These are long tunnels with a fixed central firing zone, through which trucks, bearing the wares, pass very slowly, going in cold, passing through the heat and emerging cold at the opposite end. They are the latest types used in the industry, and provide a continuous and steady form of firing (*see plate XXXIII*).

There are many variations of all the above, and also kilns with several connected chambers, both horizontally and climbing obliquely.

In selecting a kiln, the right choice for its particular purpose is very important, as a mistake may cause limitations and difficulties. Schools require small compact kilns which can be fired during a normal school day. Gas-fired muffles are very convenient, if sometimes limiting in temperature, but atmospheres, either reducing or oxidising, can be obtained quite easily in them. I have used a gas-fired, with forced draught,

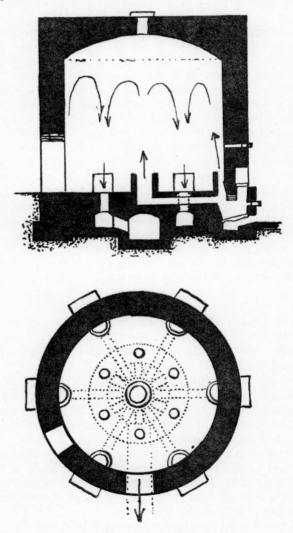

Fig. 78. Round down-draught kiln.

open flame furnace with regenerators, by Gibbons Bros., of Dudley Port, with great success. In this kiln almost any type of ware can be fired, and temperatures up to 1300° centigrade can be reached in about eight or ten hours. Oxidising or reducing atmospheres are obtainable by increasing or decreasing the air supply, and its capacity of about eighteen average size saggars, makes it possible to produce large or small pots, and of a quantity necessary for a school or institute.

KILN CONSTRUCTION

The construction of large kilns for commercial and industrial purposes is a matter for experts, and it requires considerable experience and knowledge, and also highly skilled workmanship of a specialized nature. Small kilns for schools, the individual craftsman, or for small studio pottery, can be built if attention to certain factors is carefully given. Considerable knowledge would be gained by building small and easily constructed experimental kilns.

An important problem which arises with the building of a kiln to be fired with fuel other than gas or electricity, is the chimney stack. This has a dual function—to create the necessary draught, and to conduct away the smoke and fumes ; and with regard to the latter factor, it must be borne in mind that local authorities have rules and regulations about the height of chimneys. It is advisable to find out these regulations according to the locality before beginning to build. In some cases it has been known that the cost of the chimney exceeded the cost of the kiln itself, due to the height and thickness demanded by the local authority.

The site and foundations are important, as a damp foundation will easily absorb the heat. A bed should be laid of about six to twelve inches of waterproof concrete or blue engineering bricks, and this should be insulated from the heat by a layer of insulation bricks. These are highly porous bricks produced by mixing combustible matter, such as sawdust, etc., with the clay mixture, so that when burnt, holes, or pores are left in the bricks. They are almost non-conductive of heat. Silica gravel could be used if preferred.

Side walls of kilns require about four and a half inches of insulating bricks or Kieselguhr bricks, and the crowns some two and a half to five inches of insulating material. The bricks for the different parts of the kiln must be suitable ; firebricks for the hottest parts, and ordinary bricks for those parts not directly in contact with the heat. The joints should be as thin as possible and a refractory cement—fireclay and fireclay grog—used instead of mortar, and the joints should all be broken to ensure greater strength and to prevent any cracks (which may develop when the kiln is fired) from extending. Bracings of steel bars or rods may be used to strengthen the outer walls.

The chimney should be ample and strongly built, so as not to permit the heat to escape through the walls, which would reduce the draught

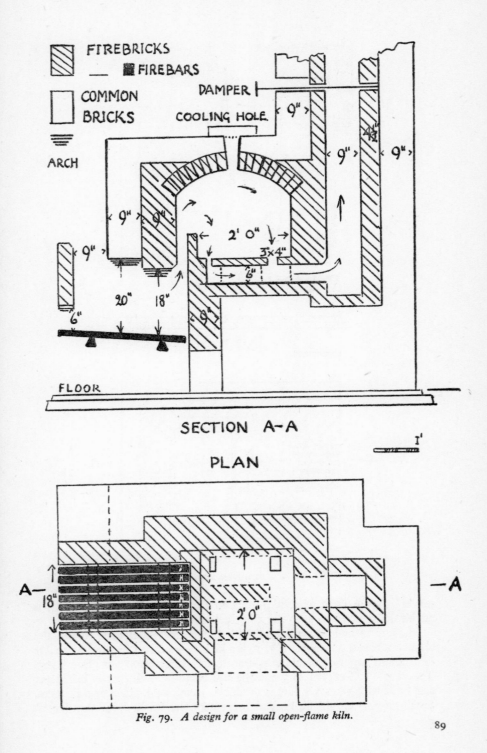

FIREBRICKS

FIREBARS

COMMON
BRICKS

ARCH

DAMPER

COOLING HOLE.

9"

4"

9"

9"

9"

9"

2' 0"

3×4"

9"

9"

6"

20"

18"

6"

9"

FLOOR

SECTION A-A

1'

PLAN

A—

18"

2' 0"

—A

Fig. 79. A design for a small open-flame kiln.

89

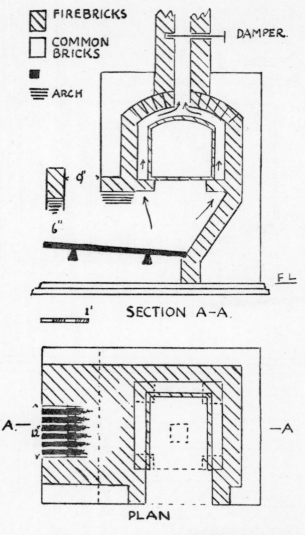

FIREBRICKS

COMMON BRICKS

ARCH

DAMPER.

SECTION A-A.

PLAN

Fig. 80. *A design for a small muffle kiln.*

power. Some form of roof protection from rain, wind, snow, etc., is advisable, in order to keep the kiln, fuel and approaches dry.

In *Figs.* 79 and 80, will be found designs for small kilns to suit the artist-craftsman or school. *Fig.* 79 is a kiln with a direct fire, quite capable of attaining any reasonable temperature for either biscuit or glaze firing. The plan is self-explanatory and the kiln could be built by any bricklayer and fired with whatever fuel is available, wood, coal, coke, or a mixture. Small saggars would be needed to protect the wares from the flames.

The following points should be observed in building this kiln ; provision should be made for a cooling hole nine inches long by four inches wide at the top of the kiln ; this could be covered with a fireclay quarry when the kiln is under fire. The arch should abut the end walls and not be built on them.

The openings in the floor, to permit the hot gases to escape and create the draught, should be four inches by one and a half inches near the bridge wall and four inches by three inches near the side wall, giving four posts. A short midfeather is built under the floor quarries to support the kiln bottom. The bridge may be formed with three inch thick fireclay quarries and the bottom flues covered with two inch thick fireclay quarries. All firebricks used for the lining of the firehole, kiln and chimney must be of suitable refractory material to withstand the high temperatures required. The doorway could be bricked up with a spy hole built in (*see Fig.* 73) and sealed with a mixture of sand and clay. Cast iron buckstaffs and tie-rods should be fixed at the corners when building, to support the kiln under fire.

Fig. 80 is a smaller muffle kiln for firing low temperature glazes and enamels, saggars being unnecessary in this type of kiln. The muffle, in one piece, is of a standard size, eighteen inches long by fourteen inches high and fourteen inches wide, obtainable from the makers of crucibles and refractories. The design permits the easy withdrawal of the muffle through the doorway, should a renewal be required. Important points in the construction are the four projecting bricks which support the muffle. The arch of the doorway should be built to touch the top edge of the muffle, in order to seal the flue around the muffle at the front.

Glossary of terms, tools, materials.

Agate ware. Onyx ware, marbled ware, pottery made to imitate these various natural materials by mixing coloured clays in strata.

Alumina. or oxide of aluminium, a constituent of clays. Pure alumina is a chemical product.

Antimony oxide. Used with lead gives yellow. Gives opacity when used with other fluxes.

Ash. Wood and plant ashes are used to give fluxes (chiefly potash and magnesia) in glazes used in the Far East.

Bag. A firebrick wall or open flue which prevents the flames from directly affecting the wares in the oven.

Ball clay. Sometimes called blue or black clay. An exceedingly plastic clay from Devon and Dorset. Forms the basis of English earthenware bodies.

Bat. Flat slabs of plaster, fireclay or clay pancake.

Baryta. Barium oxide which is produced when barium compounds are heated.

Biscuit or Bisque. Clay which has been fired once, but not glazed.

Bismuth oxide. More fusible than lead.

Bitstone. Calcined chips of flint used for placing glazed ware.

Body The mixture of clay, etc., of which the pottery is made.

Bone china. A variety of English porcelain which contains a large percentage of calcined ox bones.

Borax. Used in the composition of frits and glazes. Is a powerful flux.

Bottleneck oven. So called from its shape, usually an up-draught oven or kiln (*Fig. 77*).

Bung. A pile of ware or saggars.

Calcine. To reduce to powder by heat.

Celadon. A French name for sea green glazes on Oriental stoneware and porcelain.

Chatter. The vibrations of a turning tool when held loosely.

Chuck. A wide tapering spindle of wood or hard clay on which the pot is impaled for turning purposes.

Chum. A hollow cylinder of clay or other material used to support pots during turning.

Clamming. A mixture of sand, clay and water used to stop the cracks in the kiln door.

Cones. Seger and standard ; tall triangular pyramids made of glaze constituents. These bend and melt at various temperatures (*Fig. 72*). They are placed in the kiln where they can be seen through a mica spyhole (*Fig. 73*). See page 83.

Cornish stone. Pegmatite or Petunze. Used in bodies and glazes.

Crackle glaze. Intentional crazing used for a decorative effect.

Crazing.	Unintentional cracking of the glaze caused by the glaze not fitting the body.
Crystalline glazes.	Crystal formation in glazes.
Drawing.	Unpacking the kiln.
Earthenware.	All wares which are porous under the glaze.
Encaustic tiles.	Tiles in which the pattern is inlaid with different coloured clays.
Engobes.	Slip coatings.
Faience.	A French name for glazed earthenware. Used in England for blocks of pottery material.
Fat clay.	Highly plastic clay.
Fettle.	To trim and finish the surfaces of unfired pots.
Fireclay.	Refractory clays ; usually found below coal seams.
Fluxes.	The fusible ingredients of clays and glazes.
Frit.	Melted mixtures of silica and fluxes to render them insoluble, such as borax frit, alkaline frit, etc. Made by melting the ingredients and running out into cold water to shatter the mass to assist grinding.
Galena glaze.	Lead sulphide. An old form of lead glaze used on slip wares, obtained by dusting powdered galena over the clay piece, and firing body and glaze at one piece.
Glost fire.	The glaze fire.
Green ware.	Unfired ware.
Gres.	French for stoneware.
Grog.	Crushed or powdered burnt clay or fireclay. Used for making saggars, etc.
Hard paste.	True porcelain.
Hovel.	The bottle necked chimney which encloses the oven or kiln (*Fig.* 77).
Iron.	Oxides of—give a wide range of colours. They impart fusibility to clays ; they are carefully extracted from white bodies.
Jigger and Jolley.	Machines on which pottery shapes are made. The *jigger* is the revolving wheel head which holds the mould (*Fig.* 35). The *jolley* is the arm which holds the profile tool (*Figs.* 50-53).
Joggle.	The notch or key in a plaster mould to ensure correct registering of the parts.
Kaolin.	China clay. A fine white, pure form of clay.
Lawns.	Sieves of bronze wire for glazes and slips (*Fig.* 70).
Lustre.	A thin film of metal which gives an iridescent sheen on pottery.
Majolica.	Italian tin glazed wares, loosely applied to some soft glazes.
Marls.	Clays containing sand and lime, chiefly used for saggars, drain pipes, etc.
Master mould.	The original mould made from the model, also called the *block*.
Muffle.	The fireclay lining or box which protects the wares during firing.

Neutral.	Atmosphere between oxidation and reduction in kiln firing.
Oil spots.	Lustrous metallic spots in high temperature iron stained glazes.
Oxidation.	A plentiful supply of oxygen in the kiln firing to give complete combustion.
Parian.	A type of soft porcelain biscuit used for figures.
Pegmatite.	See Cornish stone.
Plasticity.	The essential quality of clay, enabling it to be moulded.
Placing.	Packing the pots in saggars and kilns (*Fig.* 75).
Potash.	An alkaline base used in glazes. Obtained from felspar or plant ash.
Porcelain.	Translucent pottery.
Pug mill.	A machine which makes the clay homogeneous (*plate I*).
Pyrometers.	Instruments which measure and record kiln temperatures.
Queens ware.	The cream coloured earthenware made by Josiah Wedgwood.
Reduction.	An atmosphere in the kiln caused by incomplete combustion. It reduces the metallic oxides to the metallic state.
Refractory.	Fire resisting, infusible at high temperatures.
Rouge Flambé.	Copper red glazes, produced by the reduction of copper oxides.
Rutile.	Crude oxide of titanium, is infusible and gives colours and glazes a broken effect.
Saddles.	Fired clay supports for glazed ware (*Fig.* 74).
Saggars.	Fireclay boxes of various shapes, which protect the wares during firing, and a means of packing the kiln (*Figs.* 71 *and* 75).
Sgraffito.	An Italian term meaning scratched. When the body of a pot is coated with a different coloured slip; this may be scratched or cut through revealing the body, thus giving a pattern on a different coloured ground.
Silica.	The potters' chief acid substance. Infusible by itself.
Slip.	Liquid clay.
Soda.	An alkaline base used in glazes.
Slurry.	The clay and water from the action of throwing.
Spur and Cock spurs.	Clay supports for placing glost ware. Stilts (*Fig.* 74).
Spy hole.	An observation *hole* in the kiln door or wall (*Fig.* 73).
Stanniferous glaze.	Glazes containing oxide of tin.
Stoneware.	Hard pottery usually fired above 1200° centigrade; is opaque.
Terracotta.	Reddish coloured unglazed and glazed pottery.
Weathering.	Exposing clay to the elements to improve its quality.
Wedging.	The process of cutting and slamming clay together to make it homogeneous (*Fig.* 16).

I. A vertical pug mill

II. A built-up figure group: Rolling out and preparing the figures, slabs and composite pieces

III. A built-up figure group: Sticking together the composite pieces

IV. A built-up figure group: Modelling the finishing touches

V. A built-up figure group: A close-up of the finished work

VI. Making a pressed divided dish: The model and the mould

VII. Making a pressed divided dish: Putting the pancake of clay on to the mould

VIII. Making a pressed divided dish: Trimming and smoothing the back of the dish with a potter's kidney-shaped rubber

IX. Making a pressed divided dish: Lifting the finished and dried dish off the mould

The clay centred by raising a cone

Depressing the clay cone into a cylindrical shape

X–XI. Throwing

Hollowing the cylinder

Raising the wall

XII–XIII. Throwing

*Further raising and
thinning of the wall*

*Running in the neck
of the pot*

XIV–XV. Throwing

Shaping and thinning

Cutting the pot off the wheel

XVI–XVII. Throwing

XVIII. Thrown sculpture: Composite pieces made on the wheel

XIX. Thrown sculpture: The pieces are cut to fit, then stuck together with slip

XX. Thrown sculpture: Finished and decorated by the sgraffito method

XXI. Thrown sculptures: Further work by the same method

XXII. Some animals and birds produced by the built-up methods

XXIII. A group of built-up figurines by the author

XXIV. *A thrown stoneware pot decorated with brushwork in iron oxide by the author*

XXV. Making a plate by the lever jolley, the pancake spreader is seen on the right

XXVI. Cup making with the lever jolley

XXVII. Sticking handles on to cups

XXVIII. Mould making: Pouring plaster into the case

XXIX. Slip casting: Filling the mould

XXX. A small electric kiln, school or studio size

XXXI. Placing and building-up the truck, for a truck-loading kiln

XXXII. Extracting the truck after firing

XXXIII. The tunnel oven: the loaded truck ready for firing

XXXIV. Placing glazed wares into saggars preparatory to firing

XXXV. Packing a bottle-neck oven

XXXVI. Groundlayed and painted decorations on cast and jolleyed shapes by Susie Cooper

XXXVII.   Groundlayed and scratched decorations on jolleyed shapes by Susie Cooper

XXXVIII. Lithographed decorations on jolleyed shapes by Susie Cooper

XXXIX. Resist lustre wares: Grays Pottery

XL. *Finely printed decorations by Josiah Wedgwood & Sons Ltd. Coronation mug by Eric Ravilious*
A.R.C.A.

XLI. Printed and filled-in decorations: designed by R. G. Haggar, A.R.C.A., F.R.S.A., N.R.D.

XLII. Slip wares. Devon Harvest jug decorated by the sgraffito method

DATE DUE

FEB 17

APR 1 7 2008

Demco, Inc. 38-293